THE CURTISS HAWK FIGHTERS

OTHER BOOKS BY THE SAME AUTHORS

Tracks Across the Sky
Classic Monoplanes
Aces & Planes of WW-I
Single-Engine Cessnas
Your Pilot's License

Command the Horizon
Summon the Stars
The Curtiss Hawks
Racing Planes Guide
Single-Engine Beechcrafts

THE CURTISS HAWK FIGHTERS

Page Shamburger & Joe Christy

New York
MODERN AIRCRAFT SERIES
A Division of Sports Car Press

Library of Congress Catalog Number 70-158410
ISBN 0-87112-041-0
First Printing, July 1971

MODERN AIRCRAFT SERIES

Edited by Joe Christy

A new series of popular-priced books on aircraft and their operation for everyone interested in privately owned planes. Each volume is written by an expert in the field, and is printed on fine, white paper and profusely illustrated with photographs and diagrams. Each volume $2.95.

Your Pilot's License
Your FAA Flight Exam
Legal Guide for Pilots & Owners
Your Jet Pilot Rating
Airmanship After Solo

Nav/Com Guide for Pilots
Cockpit Navigation Guide
Pilot's Weather Guide
Air Traffic Control
Instrument Flying Guide
Computer Guide

Guide to Antique Planes
Classic Biplanes
Classic Military Biplanes
Classic Monoplanes
Racing Planes Guide

Club Flying
Agricultural Aviation

Multiengine Flying
The Single-Engine Cessnas
The Piper Cub Story
The Single-Engine Beechcrafts
All About Helicopters

Hot Air Ballooning
Parachuting for Sport
Soaring Guide
Taking Pictures from the Air
Modern Aerobatics

Aces & Planes of WWI
The Curtiss Hawk Fighters
Scramble, British Aircraft WWII
Aircraft Armament

Guide to Homebuilts
Used Plane Buying Guide
Aircraft Dope & Fabric
Lightplane Construction & Repair
Lightplane Engine Guide

Published by Sports Car Press

Distributed by Crown Publishers
419 Park Avenue South, New York, N.Y. 10016

ACKNOWLEDGMENT

Material for this book was taken from the more comprehensive and definitive work, *The Curtiss Hawks,* * by the same authors, originally contracted to Wolverine Press, Inc., Kalamazoo, Michigan, for publication in hardcover at $24.95.

*©Page Shamburger and Joe Christy

CONTENTS

CONTENTS (CONTINUED)

The first Hawks were developed from the PW-8, above, which was Curtiss' first post-WW-I production fighter. It was powered with the D-12 engine of 435 hp and featured wingskin radiators (dark areas in upper wing).

Photo: Kenneth D. Wilson Collection

PART 1: THE COMPANY

Twenty-nine year-old Glenn Hammond Curtiss owned and operated the Metro Motorcycle Company in Hammondsport, New York when, in October, 1907, Dr. Alexander Graham Bell invited Curtiss to join Bell's newly-formed Aerial Experiment Association. The inventor of the telephone — who had some theories of his own about man-carrying flying machines — put up $37,000 (of his wife's money) for the construction and testing of four craft, each to be designed by one of the A.E.A.'s four active members: Canadians J.A.D. McCurdy and F.W. Baldwin; U.S. Army Lt. T.E. Selfridge, and Curtiss.

Bell chose Curtiss because of the motorcycle builder's proven ability as an engine designer, and because the Curtiss shop provided proper construction facilities. Just seven months earlier, Curtiss had become the "fastest man on earth" when he drove one of his motorcycles, powered by a Curtiss-designed engine, to a world speed record of 136.3 mph. A Curtiss engine had propelled America's first successful dirigible, the *California Arrow,* which had flown three years before; and a Curtiss engine of 20-hp was being fitted to the Baldwin non-rigid dirigible which was then under construction for the U.S. Signal Corps.

During the year and a-half the A.E.A. was in existence, four aircraft were produced, all of which flew. Curtiss' project, the *June Bug,* made its initial flight June 21, 1908; and less than two weeks later, on July 4th, Curtiss won the *Scientific American* trophy for the first official flight of more than one kilometer in the U.S.

By the time the A.E.A. was disbanded at the end of March, 1909, Curtiss had joined with Augustus M. Herring (formerly associated with Octave Chanute in gliding experiments) to form the Herring-Curtiss Company. The products of this union were the *Golden Flier,* sold to the Aeronautic Society of New York, and the *Rheims Racer* (or *Rheims Machine),* with which Curtiss won the first Gordon Bennett Cup at Rheims, France in August, 1909 (a few days after the U.S. Army took delivery of its first flying machine from the Wright brothers at Ft. Myer, Va.).

Apparently, an argument over divvying up Curtiss' air race winnings broke up the Herring-Curtiss partnership, and Curtiss, by then facing the first of several court actions brought against him by the Wrights for patent infringement,* continued with the Curtiss Aeroplane Company and produced the *Albany Flier.*

In January, 1911, while stalling a showdown with the Wrights with the first of several court appeals, Curtiss established a flying school at North Island, across the bay from San Diego, where he trained some Army aviators and made significant progress in hydroplane development.

During the next five years, Curtiss delivered about 85 aeroplanes (the word "airplane" was coined in 1916) to the U.S. Army, Navy and the export market, brought the seaplane and flying boat to a practical stage of development, and repeatedly postponed his day of legal reckoning with the Wrights.

During this time, Curtiss engine development proceeded apace with the improved airframes. With his motorcycle and dirigible powerplants (two and four-cylinder air-cooleds) as background, Curtiss had designed a 30-hp air-cooled V-8 for his A.E.A. *June Bug,* and a 50-hp water-cooled V-8 for his *Rheims Racer* in 1909. In 1911, he sold the Navy its first airplane which was fitted with a Curtiss water-cooled V-8 Model O of 70-hp; and by 1914, the Model O engine had progressed through the Model OX, OX-2, etc., to the 90-hp OX-5.

Curtiss farmed out most of the actual construction of his engines, with the Kirkham brothers of nearby Bath, N.Y., doing much of the

---

*The Wright brothers' principal patent covered their system of lateral control, wing-warping. Curtiss used hinged ailerons, developed (and named) by the Frenchman Esnault-Pelterie, in 1905; but the Wrights — and the courts — held that ailerons were merely another form of wing-warping based upon the same aerodynamic discovery.

machining and assembling. Curtiss also had, by 1911, some excellent mechanics on his payroll, and these men, too, contributed much to Curtiss engine design. For example, it was Henry Kleckler who re-designed the rocker arm assembly of the Model O engine to produce the Model OX. And Charles Kirkham did so much work on the OX-5 that he eventually accepted credit (or blame, if you prefer) for that engine's design.

Charles Kirkham's most important achievment however was design of a V-12 liquid-cooled engine of 400-hp, the K-12, which he laid down in 1916 for Curtiss. After WW-I, this powerplant, de-bugged and refined under the direction of Curtiss Chief Motor Engi-neer, F.R. Porter, became the D-12 and powered many early Hawks. A scaled-up version of the D-12 (with re-designed cylinders), develop-ed by Arthur Nutt, was called the *Conqueror,* and this 600-hp engine, which appeared in 1927, was fitted to later Hawks. But that is taking us ahead of our story.

In 1916, the war in Europe was two years old and by then the role of the airplane, as an instrument of war, had come into focus. Therefore, investment money in America began looking with favor upon its miniscule aircraft industry. Automobile makers in particular were attracted to the building of airplanes because they quite natural-ly (though erroneously) regarded such an activity as only slightly different than the mass production of cars. Orville Wright (Wilbur died of typhoid fever in 1912) had sold out to a combine of invest-ment banders which controlled the Simplex Automobile Company in 1915; and Curtiss, eager for the kind of capital the auto interests could provide, allowed John North Willys of Willys Car Company to bring in a financial expert, C.M. Keys, to re-organize Curtiss' holdings and market securities. Thus, Willys became a major stock-holder in the new Curtiss Aeroplane and Motor Corporation, Keys a vice-president, and Glenn Curtiss ended up as president of the Engi-neering Division, established at Garden City, N.Y., and board chair-man of the parent organization. A new plant was also obtained at Buffalo, N.Y., and after entry of the U.S. into WW-I — April 6, 1917 — this facility was greatly expanded and Curtiss Aeroplane & Motor became the most important aircraft builder in the nation.

During the first World War, the company's principal products were the JN-4 "Jenny" trainer for the Army (designed by B. Douglas Thomas, formerly with Sopwith and AVRO in England), the N-9 Navy trainer, which was essentially a Jenny on floats with bigger wings, and a couple of flying boat models.

But Curtiss tried fighter* airplane designs soon after the corporation was organized, and though none were entirely successful until the first Hawk appeared in 1924, it is accurate to say that Curtiss fighters were offered in an un-broken line for more than thirty years — 1916 through 1947.

The first Curtiss design of this type was the triplane Scout, S-3, that appeared in 1916. It was powered with an OXX-2 engine of 100-hp, and four were built. One example of the CB *Battler* followed, along with a couple of craft almost lost to present day researchers and of which little is known at this writing. Next came the Model HA *Dunkirk Fighter* of 1918 of which three were built; and then the Model 18-T triplane fighter for the Navy. The 18-T, also called the Curtiss *Wasp,* was the test bed for the K-12 engine.

By 1920, John N. Willys was willing to take his wartime profits and sell his Curtiss holdings. Therefore, Clement M. Keys, the corporation's original financial architect, gained control of Curtiss Aeroplane & Motor, forseeing the day when it would be the keystone of a great aviation empire.

Keys was a Canadian and a former history professor who came to New York in 1903 as an editor of the *Wall Street Journal,* moved to Walter Hines Page's† influential *World's Work* as financial editor, and then into investment banking before Willys called upon him to put together Curtiss Aeroplane & Motor in 1916.

In 1923, encouraged by the success of the Curtiss military racers, powered with the excellent D-12 engine (developed from Kirkham's K-12), Keys re-organized under the name "Curtiss Aeroplane and Motor Company, Inc.," and concentrated upon finding — and stimulating — markets for Curtiss military aircraft. Glenn Curtiss remained in the company as board chairman and president of the Engineering Division. And we should add that the wartime patent pool, and the organization of both Wright and Curtiss interests into public corporations, had meanwhile drained the vigor from the Wright lawsuits and this issue eventually died quietly of malnutrition.

Meanwhile, the Curtiss military racers — of which nine were built, 1921-1925 inclusive — did much to enhance the reputation of

---

*The U.S. Army never did officially accept the term "fighter" for its fighter aircraft. Its first planes of this type were "Scouts." Then, until the U.S. Air Force was born in 1947 as a separate service, such craft were "Pursuits."

†Walter Hines Page (co-author Page Shamburger's great uncle) was U.S. Ambassador to Britain during WW-I.

Curtiss airplanes, and established the 435-hp D-12 (V-1150) as the best liquid-cooled aircraft engine in its class. During their short careers, the Army and Navy Curtiss racers won the Pulitzer Trophy four times, the International Schneider Trophy for seaplane racers twice, and established a world's landplane speed record for good measure.

So, with the D-12 engine (which was lighter, smaller, more flexible and far more reliable than the famed 400-hp Liberty of WW-I — a boondoggle foisted upon the Army and Navy by politically powerful automobile interests via the wartime Aircraft Production Board) promising much improved performance for a new generation of fighter planes, Curtiss engineers, headed by William E. Gilmore, produced the PW-8 — a double-bay biplane fighter with wing-skin radiators — in 1923. The Air Service* soon purchased 28 of these machines.

But meanwhile, in July, 1924, just as PW-8 deliveries were beginning, Boeing came up with its new XPW-9, a D-12-powered single-bay biplane fighter with tapered wings which, in comparative tests at Selfridge Field, Michigan, seemed superior to the PW-8. So, William Gilmore, in anticipation of the official competition scheduled for September — at the Army's air research and test center, Dayton, Ohio — modified a PW-8 into a single-bay biplane with five feet less wingspan and substituted a tunnel radiator beneath the nose for the aerodynamically-clean but leak-prone wing-skin PW-8 radiator. This resulted in the XPW-8A.

In the September competition, the XPW-8A proved faster and possessed a better climb-rate than the XPW-9, but it was less maneuable, a fatal deficiency for a fighter aircraft. Therefore, aware that the Air Service was leaning toward the XPW-9 (actually, both designs were accepted by the Army in order to encourage continued development of military aircraft by both companies), Bill Gilmore again managed to obtain a grace period in which to re-work the Curtiss fighter.

Gilmore took his plane back to Buffalo and charged young George A. Page, Jr. with the task of quickly laying out a new set of tapered wings for it. The resulting aircraft was called the XPW-8B and it was

---

*The U.S. Army Air Service became the U.S. Army Air Corps July 2, 1926, following Congressional approval of the Air Corps Act. With increased autonomy under General "Hap" Arnold it became the U.S. Army Air Forces (USAAF) June 20, 1941. Today's independent U.S. Air Force (USAF) was created by the National Security Act of 1947 which became effective September 18th of that year. The Navy's Bureau of Aeronautics was established August 10, 1921.

a winner. In production for the Air Service, it became the P-1 — the first Hawk.*

Army Aircraft Designations: Throughout WW-I and into 1919, the Army Air Service and Naval Air Service used the manufacturer's model number for aircraft identification. In 1920, the Army adopted a type-model-series system of letter and number designations. This system classified all planes acquired from that time according to mission; "B" for bombers, "P" for pursuit, etc. (older aircraft still in service such as the JN-6, DH-4, retained original designations). This first letter, designating basic type, was supplemented until 1924 by a second "descriptive" letter, and this resulted in the "PW" designation (as in PW-8, PW-9), meaning "Pursuit, Water-cooled," or "PN" meaning "Pursuit, Night" (the Curtiss PN-1, an early night fighter). These letters were followed by a number indicating the model within that type; for example, PW-8, which was the eighth water-cooled pursuit proposed or built since 1920 for the Army. Finally, a series letter followed the model number to identify variants of a basic model, such as the PW-8A.

The use of the prefix "X" to denote the experimental status of an aircraft was begun in 1924, and XPW-8B is an example.

Beginning with the first Hawk, ordered early in 1925, use of the two-letter designator began to fade and only the "P" for pursuit was employed, while the model number started over with "1," although some two-letter designators (PB-2, for instance) were used into the thirties.

In 1929, the "Y" designator was added to indicate an aircraft in service test status when a limited number of a new type were sent to regular duty squadrons for evaluation.

Navy Aircraft Designations: The U.S. Navy's first Hawk, which was essentially the same as the Army's P-1, carried the designation F6C-1. That meant it was a fighter (F), the 6th type (6) built by Curtiss (C), and the first model of that design (-1). It followed the F5C-1, of course (or XF5C-1 as it was retroactively called), an XPW-8 obtained from the Army and fitted with an early radial engine, the Wright P-1 (Students of early Curtiss history still disagree as to whether this transfer was actually made or was merely a proposal. Your authors could find no mention of an F5C in either Navy or Curtiss files). Before that, there had been the F4C's, Curtiss-built versions of the earlier

*It's true that the Curtiss company retroactively called the PW-8's "Straight-Wing Hawks," after the P-1 appeared; but almost no one else ever did. To the pilots who flew them during their short service lives, PW-8's were simply PW-8's.

and tiny TS-1 Navy fighter; and preceding the F4C's were the Curtiss Navy racers, CR-1 through R3C series, which were actually carried in Navy inventory as F1C through F3C, probably to justify their costs to an economy-minded Congress.

The Navy did not adopt the "X" for experimental craft until 1927. Therefore, earlier Navy experimental aircraft that show up in the records with this designation, received it retroactively.

Hawk P-1B just off assembly line at Curtiss-Buffalo. Army Air Corps purchased 25 P-1B's, delivered late in 1926.

Photo: Francis H. Dean Collection

PART 2: HAWK BIPLANES

U.S. Army

The Army bought a total of 247 Hawk biplanes from 1925 to 1932 inclusive. These included 36 models and variants. Except for the XP-10, a Conqueror-powered craft with gulled wings and wing-skin radiators, which was an all-new design (and unsuccessful), all the rest were modified versions of the basic P-1 or P-6 airframes.

The significant difference between the P-6 series and earlier Hawks was the advance to the 600-hp Conqueror engine and ethylene glycol (Prestone) coolant. Prestone radiators not only solved some operational problems involving engine coolant temperature control (ethylene glycol has both much lower freezing point and higher boiling point than water), but could be made much smaller, allowing airframe re-design of improved aerodynamic efficiency, while also providing an important weight reduction with lesser amount of coolant required.

The first Hawk order from the Air Service was for fifteen airplanes. This included the XP-1, s/n 25-410, nine P-1's and five P-2's. The XP-1 went to McCook Field, the Army's air research and test center, and remained there as an engine test bed. It was raced in 1926, fitted with an inverted air-cooled Liberty engine; and it became the XP-17 in 1930 with installation of an experimental Curtiss v-1460 inverted air-cooled V-12 engine of 500-hp.

The nine P-1 Hawks, fitted with Curtiss V-1150 (D-12) engines, saw service with the 27th and 94th Pursuit Squadrons of the First Pursuit Group at Selfridge Field, Michigan.

The P-2's were P-1 airframes powered with the new Curtiss V-1400 engine of 600-hp. P-2 s/n 25-420 was painted red, equipped with a side-mounted supercharger and sent to McCook where it was designated XP-2. Curtiss claimed that it was the fastest pursuit plane in the world at 20,000 feet in 1927; but the V-1400 engine contained too many bugs and the four P-2's in squadron service were converted into a pair of P-1's with D-12 engines (24-421 and 424), a P-1A with a D-12A (422), and an XP-6 with the new V-1550 Conqueror engine (423).

In April, 1926, delivery of 25 P-1A's began. These were powered with the D-12C which had an improved fuel system, and these craft saw service with the 17th, 27th and 94th Pursuit Squadrons* and the 43rd School Squadron at Kelly Field.

P-1A s/n 26-300, delivered in October, 1926, was immediately given a new radial engine of about 400-hp (Curtiss records say 390-hp in one place; 405-hp in another) and re-designated the XP-3. This engine was the R-1454 developed by Curtiss from Army specifications based upon the Wright R-1 of 1920. It was not successful and a new Pratt & Whitney Wasp of similar power was put in the XP-3 making it the XP-3A. Later, when this same airframe was used to test the smaller Wasp Jr engine (which began at 300-hp and grew to 450-hp), the result was the XP-21A. And if you think this is confusing, hang on; we're just getting started.

Twenty-five P-1B's were ordered in August, 1926, and the first was delivered in November of that year. The P-1B Hawk had a new radiator, flares and other, minor improvements. It served with the 27th mostly; six went to Wright Field (which replaced McCook during the winter of 1926-27) while the 17th and 94th got three apiece.

Also in August of 1926, the Air Corps decided to try a smaller engine in the Hawk airframe and employ the resulting craft as an advanced trainer at Kelly Field. The prototype was called the XAT-4 and was a P-1A airframe fitted with the Wright-built Hispano-Suiza

---

*The First Pursuit Group was the only such group in the Air Service ("Air Corps" after July, 1926) until 1930. It was activated at Selfridge Field, Mt. Clemmons, Michigan, in August, 1919, and was originally made up of the 27th, 94th, 95th and 147th Aero Squadrons. In 1921, the 147th became the 17th; and a year later, when the designation "Aero Squadron" was dropped, all became "Pursuit Squadrons." The 95th moved to March Field, Riverside, California in 1927.

The P-1C Hawk had a modified aft turtle deck and no headrest. This one, s/n 29-238 of the 17th Pursuit Squadron, was wrecked in a landing accident March 26, 1929.

Photo: Robert Cavanagh

V-8 of 180-hp. Thirty-five production AT-4's were delivered with the Wright-Hispano Model E engine* of 204-hp; but performance was so poor (122 mph top speed), all AT-4's were soon given new D-12 engines and those planes, re-designated P-1D's, remained at Kelly Field, many serving as late as 1932.

Between July and September of 1927, five AT-5's were also received by the 43rd School Squadron at Kelly. These were P-1A airframes fitted with Wright J-5 Whirlwind engines of 220-hp; but these craft, too, were soon given 435-hp D-12 engines and then redesignated P-1E's.

The next Air Corps Hawk, delivered during the early part of 1928, was the P-5, called the Superhawk by Curtiss. It was powered with the D-12F engine (heavier crankshaft) boosted by a side-mounted F-2 supercharger, a combination that gave the Superhawk a top speed of 173 mph at 25,000 feet and a service ceiling of 31,000. The P-5 had a rigid landing gear with oleo shocks built into each wheel. One P-5 went to Wright Field; two were wrecked very quickly, and

---

*The Wright Aeronautical Corporation was organized in 1919 from the liquidated remains of the WW-I Wright-Martin Company, principally with a license to build the French Hispano-Suiza — "Hisso" — engines (originally designed by a Swiss, Marc Birkigt). Wright Aeronautical's boss was Frederick B. Rentschler until late 1924 when he quit to form Pratt & Whitney. Wright Aeronautical and Curtiss Aeroplane & Motor merged in 1929 to form Curtiss-Wright Aeronautical Corporation.

Hawk Model AT-5A was powered with Wright Whirlwind engine and intended for training. Most were later given D-12 engines and re-designated P-1F's.

Photo: Merle C. Olmsted Collection

two remained in service with the 94th until April, 1932, providing service experience with turbo-superchargers.

Meanwhile, the 43rd at Kelly needed more pursuit trainers, so 31 AT-5A's were ordered early in 1928. These were P-1B airframes with Wright J-5 engines. And — you guessed it — 24 AT-5A's were soon given D-12 engines, making them P-1F's. Seven remained AT-5A's; and almost all P-1F's remained at Kelly.

Delivered at approximately the same time as the AT-5A's were five similar Hawks powered with the P&W R-1340-3 Wasp of 425-hp. These were P-3A's, and all went to Selfridge.

The P-1C Hawk was the last of the P-1 production series. Thirty-three were ordered in October, 1928, and all were delivered during the first four months of 1929. Most served with the First Pursuit Group at Selfridge; some went to Kelly late in life. The first three P-1C's were equipped with oleo shock absorber landing gears, according to Curtiss records.

The first "P-6" Hawks weren't really P-6's. These were a pair of craft used to prove the new Conqueror V-1570 engine (developed from the first Conqueror, the V-1550). These planes were raced in the unlimited class at the 1927 National Air Races held at Felts Field, Spokane, Washington, and took first and second place. One of these airplanes was the P-2 (s/n 25-423) which first became the XP-6 when given a V-1550 Conqueror. The other, called the XP-6A, would have been better described perhaps as the "XPW-8C," because it was essentially the same airplane as the XPW-8A with a Conqueror engine. It had the XPW-8A's single-bay constant-chord wings complete with wing-skin radiators. Its fuselage, tail and landing gear were furnished by P-1A s/n 26-295. Its Conqueror was a special high compression engine which burned 80% benzol and 20% av-gas. Contrary to previously published descriptions, it was direct drive (not geared) and developed 675 hp at 2,400 rpms. This airplane, flown by Lt. Eugene Batten, easily won the *Spokane Spokesman-Review* Trophy with an average speed of 201.2 mph. Lt. A.J. Lyon in the XP-6 took second place with 189.6 mph.

Although neither the XP-6 nor the XP-6A were P-6 prototypes, these craft did, apparently, help sell the Air Corps on the new P-6 series which were Conqueror-powered, with the standard Hawk wings and tail, and a fuselage rounded-off and filled out with extra formers and stringers. The Air Corps budget for fiscal 1929 earmarked $247,405 for 18 P-6 airframes and $380,905 for 36 V-1570 engines

The XP-6D Hawk, pictured July 3, 1929, with its pilot, Capt. Ross Hoyt who flew it to Nome, Alaska from New York in 38 hours. Engine was the 600-hp Curtiss Conqueror.

Photo: National Air & Space Museum

with spares. This broke down to $13,744.73 for each airframe and $10,590 per engine.*

Meanwhile, the last P-1C, s/n 29-259, delivered in April, 1929, was fitted with a Conqueror engine and fuselage tanks, stretching its fuel capacity to 250 glalons, to make the XP-6B. Popularly called both the "Hoyt Special" and the "Nomelaska," it was flown by Capt. Ross G. Hoyt from Mitchel Field, New York, to Nome (with five fuel stops) in 34 hours and 20 minutes flying time in July, 1929. Attempting the return flight, Hoyt flipped it onto its back in an emergency landing after engine failure due to contaminated fuel.

Delivery of the real P-6's began in October, 1929, and ten machines of the 18-plane order had gone to the Air Corps five months later when production was stopped. Tests with ethylene glycol at Wright Field had established that its heat transfer properties would allow a 50% reduction in radiator area and save about 50 pounds in weight, because 10 gallons of Prestone would provide the same cooling for a Conqueror as 15-18 gallons of water.

Therefore, the P-6, s/n 29-262, became the first P-6A when given a small radiator and Prestone cooling system — after which the last eight planes of the original P-6 order were completed as P-6A's.

Two additional P-6A's were added to this total when a pair of craft ordered as P-11's (s/n 29-367-368) were finished at the factory as P-6A's after planned Curtiss Chieftain engine installations were abandoned.

Later, all of the earlier P-6's were converted to P-6A's, except for s/n 29-261 which was wrecked shortly after delivery.

In 1931, P-6 s/n 29-260, by that time a P-6A, was given a supercharger and re-designated XP-6D. After a leisurely test of this machine, ten more P-6A's were converted to P-6D's, along with the two P-11/P-6A's. This made a total of twelve P-6D's — because the XP-6D (Wright Field plane #XP-580) was returned to P-6A configuration.

Meanwhile, the third production P-6A, s/n 29-262, was removed from service with the First Pursuit Group and returned to Curtiss for extensive modification. Re-designated the XP-22, its radiator frontal area was cut, lowering coolant capacity to 8.36 gallons, and positioned farther aft. For a time, the XP-22 wore a strange, egg-shaped ring cowl to smooth and direct air flow to the radiator. Then a round ring cowl, within which the radiator was contained, was

*Price of the direct-drive unsupercharged Conqueror V-1570 was down to $6,952.17 in August, 1932. The V-1150 D-12, which sold for $9,000 during the early twenties, was down to $4,852.50 for the D-12E by 1932.

Original configuration of Al Williams' famed Gulfhawk (NX-982V) was same as the export P-6S Model; a Cyclone-powered P-6 airframe. Pictured is Williams' plane which was delivered with a British-built Jupiter engine. Later, much modified.

Photo: Francis H. Dean Collection

Hawk P-6D of the 37th Attack Squadron.

Photo: Merle C. Olmsted Collection

Hawk P-6E of the 17th Pursuit Squadron; Capt Ross Hoyt Flying.

Photo: USAF

tried (which made the XP-22 look like a radial-engined craft), but finally these experiments were abandoned, the radiator returned to its place beneath the rear of the engine, the nose was re-designed and a new single-strut landing gear installed. The result was a prototype of the P-6E.

We say "a prototype" because there were really two of them, and the plane officially designated XP-6E was another machine. After tests of the XP-22 were completed in July, 1931, the single-strut landing gear and everything from the firewall forward was removed from the XP-22 and installed on the YP-20 Hawk, whereupon the YP-20 became the XP-6E.

The YP-20 began life as P-11 s/n 29-374, but was converted on the production line to the YP-20 when the original Curtiss R-1640 Chieftain engine proved unacceptable and it received instead a Wright R-1820 Cyclone. Along with the Cyclone the YP-20 was also fitted with a steerable tail wheel in place of a skid and given a taller vertical fin at the expense of some rudder balance area. So, when fitted with the P-6E components from the XP-22, the YP-20 turned-XP-6E was very close to the final P-6E configuration — except for a slightly deeper fuselage and shorter headrest.

On July 24, 1931, the Air Corps approved an order for 45

Y1P-22's. This designation was briefly changed to P-6C, but by then the XP-6E had taken to the air at Wright Field and the designation P-6E was firmed up before the planes were delivered, beginning in December, 1931.

The first P-6E, s/n 32-233, went to Wright Field for official performance tests, then back to the factory from which it re-emerged in April, 1933, as the XP-6H, a six-gun fighter. In addition to its standard armament — a pair of .30 calibers, or one .30 and one .50 caliber, mounted just beneath the exhaust stacks on each side — it also had a pair of .30 calibers in the top wing and one in each lower wing, all four firing outside the propeller arc.

All of the remaining 44 airplanes went to the 17th and 94th Pursuit Squadrons originally; although the 17th and 94th soon gave up ten P-6E's to the 33rd Pursuit Squadron of the Eighth Pursuit Group, which had been activated in April, 1931, at Langley Field, Va.

Effective service life of the P-6E's ended in October, 1937, following a Wright Field directive that placarded them against spins. On February 28, 1939, an order from the office of the Chief of Air Corps directed that the 17 P-6E's and one XP-6H still around (at Maxwell Field, Alabama) be surveyed or transferred to Classification 25. Therefore, between May and September that year, all were donated to tech schools for classroom training. The only known example remaining today is at the Air Force Museum, Wright-Patterson AFB, Ohio. It is s/n 32-261. It was restored over a three-year period by students of Purdue University's Aviation Technology Department under the direction of Professor Ernest Blatchley.

The last Hawk biplane design tested by the Air Corps was the XP-23. Ordered on the same contract with the P-6E's, it could hardly be called a modified P-6E. It was an all-new design. True, its fabric-covered wings retained the Clark Y airfoil and exact shape and dimensions of previous Hawk wings; but they were re-designed internally by Curtiss engineer Edwin C. Walton and were framed from metal spars and ribs in place of wood. The XP-23 also possessed a completely new all-metal fuselage of monocoque construction, new tail surfaces, new landing gear and a geared GIV-1570C Conqueror with side-mounted turbo-supercharger. It was a beautiful machine, with even cleaner lines than the last of Britain's best biplane fighters, the Hawker *Spanish Fury* which followed three years later. But the XP-23, which went to the Air Corps in late February, 1932 (along with P-6E deliveries), appeared too late and offered too little in increased performance to stave off the inevitable displacement of the biplane as a first-line Air Corps fighter. Less than a month later, the

Hawk YP-23, powered with Conqueror GIV-1570-M engine, resulted when turbo supercharger and three-blade prop were removed from the XP-23. Last biplane fighter design evaluated by the Air Corps.

first all-metal low-wing Army fighter, the Boeing P-26 (XP-936 in prototype) took to the air with its promise of 230 mph; and the XP-23, which could do but 223 mph at 15,000 feet, never really had a chance. With its three-blade prop and supercharger removed, the XP-23 was re-classified to service test status as the YP-23 for a time. Then it was returned to Curtiss where it was dismantled, its wings later turning up on the Navy's XF11C-1 Hawk.

Curtiss D-12 (V-1150) Engine:
Type: Twelve-cylinder, water-cooled, 60-degree V with two rows of six cylinder cast *en bloc* and bolted to crankcase. The closed-top, steel cylinder sleeves were screwed into the aluminum heads which were bolted to the block. Valve seats were machined in top. Aluminum heads contained valve ports and guides and supported the camshafts. There were four valves per cylinder actuated by a pair of overhead camshafts for each block of cylinders, and these were driven by radial shafts at the rear of each cylinder block. Pistons were trunk type of aluminum alloy.

Weight .... 680 lbs dry
Dimensions .... 56-¾ in long; 34-¾ in high; 24-¼ in wide
Normal output at 2,300 rpms, early models .... 435 hp
Normal output at 2,300 rpms, late models .... 460 hp
Normal fuel consumption .... 38 gph

24

Curtiss Conqueror (V-1550 and V-1570) Engines

Type: Twelve-cylinder, liquid-cooled, 60-degree V with *en bloc* cast cylinders. The Conqueror was made in both geared and direct-drive versions. Compression ratios varied from 5.9:1 to 8.3:1 as fuels improved and more efficient cooling developed. Originally run at 1,550 cubic inches displacement and 575 hp, it was soon upped to 1,570 cubic inches and 600 hp at 2,400 rpms at sea level. It was developed by Arthur Nutt from the D-12, and its crankcase, crankshaft and connecting rods were almost identical to those of the D-12, though crankshaft diameter was increased from three inches to three and a-half inches. The Conqueror's cylinders differed from those of the D-12 in that the cylinder sleeve was open at both ends, screwed into the aluminum head, and its larger valves seated on aluminum-bronze inserts in the head. Frontal area of the Conqueror was about two inches narrower than that of the D-12 as a result of re-design of the overhead cam shaft drives.

Weight .... 750 lbs dry
Dimensions ....61-¼ in long; 25-5/16 in wide
Bore and Stroke .... 5-⅛ in; 6-¼ in respectively
Normal fuel consumption .... 56 gph

ARMY BIPLANE HAWKS, SPECIFICATIONS & PERFORMANCE

	P-1	P-1B	P-1C	P-6A	P-6D	P-6E	XP-6F
Wing span (ft & in)	31′ 6″	31′ 6″	31′ 6″	31′ 6″	31′ 6″	31′ 6″	31′ 6″
Wing span, lower	25′ 11½″	25′ 11½″	25′ 11½″	25′ 11½″	25′ 11½″	25′ 11½″	25′ 11½″
Length	22′ 10″	22′ 11″	22′ 11½″	23′ 7″	23′ 7″	23′ 2″	23′ 00″
Gross weight (lbs)	2,846	2,841	2,974	3,172	3,483	3,436	3,842
Empty weight	2,046	2,041	2,137	2,692	2,865	2,677	3,027
Power loading	6.5lbs/hp	6.5	6.8	5.3	5.8	5.7	6.4
Fuel capacity (gal)	100*	100*	100*	100*	100*	100*	100*
Max. speed (mph)	163	165	160	176.8+	197‡	193	212+
Landing speed	59	58.7	59.4	60	62	61	64
Rate of Climb (fpm)	1,315	1,600	1,540	2,350	2,270	2,460	2,100
Service Ceiling	21,000	21,000	21,400	27,200	31,000	23,900	
Absolute Ceiling	22,500	22,300	22,900	28,400		24,900	
Range at .8 max rpm	350 mi	342 mi	328 mi	256 mi	280 mi	272 mi	

* 50 gal internal fuselage tank plus 50 gal jettisonable belly tank

* 100 gal internal

+ at 10,000 ft

‡ at 13,000 ft

Maximum speeds at sea level except as noted; climb rates are maximum initial.

U.S. Navy and Marine Corps

The U.S. Navy's first Hawk, which was the same as the Army's P-1, carried the designation F6C-1. Nine were ordered in January,

The Navy's F6C-1 Hawk was essentially the same as the Army's P-1. Pictured is one of five delivered to Fighting Squadron Two in August, 1925.

Photo: U.S. Navy

1925; but only five were delivered the following August (to Fighting Squadron 2), while the remaining four were converted at the factory with a new landing gear for carrier operation and re-designated F6C-2's. This gear included a spreader bar fitted with metal guides that engaged transverse wires on the deck of the Langley* and insured a straight run. This system was discontinued in 1927 when the Navy's second and third carriers were commissioned.

Two of the original F6C-1's were later converted to F6C-3's, while another became the prototype of the F6C-4. This left but two F6C-1's (s/n A-6969 and 6971), which were transferred to the Marines, VF-10M, in 1927, and remained in the Corps for the rest of their service lives.

The four F6C-2's, delivered in November, 1925, were mixed with other carrier-based fighters in service such as the Boeing F2B's

*Until the carriers Saratoga and Lexington were commissioned in November and December, 1927, the U.S. had only the Langley, converted from the collier Jupiter, which entered service in 1922. After the Lex and Sara, came the Ranger, in June, 1937 (a year after the inadequate Langley had been converted to a seaplane tender), and then the Enterprise, commissioned in May, 1938. The Wasp was commissioned in April, 1940, and the Hornet in October, 1941. America entered WW-II with these seven carriers.

and F3B's as well as the Hawk F6C-3's. The F6C-2's finished their Navy careers with Lt. Cmdr. F.D. Wagner's VF-2 Squadron at North Island in 1928, then went to the Marine's VF-9M.

Thirty-five F6C-3's — production models of the F6C-2 built with P-1A airframes and equipped with the D-12 engine with an improved fuel system — were delivered to the Navy during 1927. Two additional F6C-3's resulted from the conversions of F6C-1's s/n A-6970 and A-6972. These craft originally equipped Fighting Squadron Five (VF-5), and Light Bombing Squadron One (VB-1B), the latter operating its F6C-3's as seaplanes mounted on twin floats for a time. Altogether, a total of 17 F6C-3's were assigned to Marine squadrons, with another seven going to VF-9M (Fighting Nine had been VF-1M until July, 1927); six went to VJ-6M ("J" for utility), and four to VF-10M.

By the time the F6C-3's were delivered, however, the Navy had already decided to switch to air-cooled engines for all shipboard type aircraft. The success of the new Pratt & Whitney R-1340 Wasp clinched that decision. The Wasp engine had first flown in May, 1926, and the Navy — which had fostered its development — was so pleased with its performance an order for 200 Wasps was placed in October, 1926.

Meanwhile, the first F6C-1, s/n A-6968, was fitted with a Wasp Model A of 400-hp (official military rating at 1,900 rpms), and re-designated the F6C-4 (it was not the "XF6C-4" because the Navy didn't adopt "X" for experimental category until 1927). This proved a happy combination for Navy needs and 31 production models were ordered.

The production F6C-4 Hawks also possessed a new landing gear with a two-piece spreader-bar anchored to a center V-strut. Deliveries began in February, 1927, with four planes going to the Marines' VF-10M, and most of the others going to the Navy's Fighting Two. Later, Marine Squadrons VF-8M and VF-9M had the dash-fours. During 1930, VF-2 (the "Fighting Chiefs;" largely made up of Naval aviators of chief petty officer rank) operated from the Langley until about mid-year when they returned to North Island and gave up their F6C-4's, sending nine to Pensacola and the rest to VF-10M.

Now, the Curtiss Aeroplane & Motor Company had no air-cooled engine to match the new P&W R-1340 Wasp in 1926. Arthur Nutt and friends had been half-heartedly working on the 400-hp R-1454 under an Army development contract, but abandoned it in October, 1926, after it proved inferior to the Wasp when tested in

A Hawk F6C-4 of VF-9M Squadron. Thirty-one of this Wasp-powered model were delivered to the Navy in 1927.

Photo: USMC via Rowland P. Gill

The P&W Wasp-powered F7C-1 Seahawk served with the Marines. In cockpit of second production model is Temple Joyce, Curtiss test pilot, later a principal in the Berliner-Joyce Aircraft Company.

Photo: U.S. Navy

the Army's XP-3 Hawk. Therefore, on December 8, 1926, Curtiss Contracted to design an all-new shipboard Navy fighter that would be Wasp-powered. The XF7C-1 Seahawk emerged from that effort and was first flown by Curtiss test pilot Temple Joyce* on February 28, 1927.

This prototype Seahawk, s/n A-7653, at first had a straight one-piece upper wing, but that was quickly changed to a constant-chord wing with seven-degrees of sweepback outboard of a 96-inch center section. Span was 30 ft 8 in upper; 28 ft lower, and airfoil was the Curtiss C-72. The XF7C-1 landing gear consisted of two vees hinged to bottom fuselage longerons and two half-axels hinged to a V-cabane under the fuselage. Oleo shocks were contained within each individual wheel, along with hydraulic brakes. Gross weight was 2,655 lbs; top speed at sea level was 157.6 mph, and initial climb rate slightly over 2,000 fpm. The third production craft was briefly fitted with leading edge wing slats. The Navy bought the prototype August 28,1927, but waited another year before ordering 17 production models which were delivered in December, 1928 and January, 1929. All apparently went to VF-5M, then at Quantico, after head rests and P-6 landing gears were installed and prop spinners discarded. The F7C-1's remained at Quantico with VF-9M through 1933, and were the last Hawks owned by the Marines.

In 1930, Hawk F6C-3, s/n A-7147, was returned to Curtiss and totally rebuilt during the summer into a pure racer, a parasol mono-plane with Conqueror engine, single-strut landing gear and wing-skin radiators. It was re-designated XF6C-6† and, with Marine Capt. Arthur Page at the controls, was entered in the Thompson Trophy race held at Chicago's Curtiss-Reynolds Airport on Septem-ber 1. Page averaged 219 mph for 17 of the five-mile laps around the 100-mile course before he was overcome by carbon monoxide fumes from his engine. He was well ahead of all other contestants when he pulled up sharply in a climbing turn above the infield just short of the home pylon, then plummeted to the ground. He died

---

*Temple N. Joyce, a WW-I pilot, represented the French Morane-Saulnier com-pany in America until he joined Curtiss in 1925. He left Curtiss in 1927 to become a Chance Vought vice-president; later teamed up with Henry A. Berliner to form the Berliner-Joyce Aircraft Company of Alexandria, Va.

†The XF6C-5 designation had been given to F6C-1 s/n A-6968 when, after serving as the prototype for the F6C-4's, it was fitted with a P&W R-1690 Hornet engine for test. The designation F6C-6 had been applied to F6C-3 s/n A-7144, modified for the 1929 Thompson race in which it placed fourth with Cmdr. J.J. Clark flying.

the next day.

Perhaps we should also note that the award for the "Most Meritorious Flying" at the 1930 Chicago races went to Al Williams for his aerobatic artistry in his new Curtiss Gulfhawk. Williams' Gulfhawk was originally a P-6 airframe with Cyclone R-1820-53 engine, which made it a cross between the export models P-6S and Hawk II. However, Williams took delivery of the plane fitted with a British-built 800hp Jupiter radial engine. He cracked it up in Miami after an engine failure, and then gave it the first of several extensive re-builds it was to suffer during its long life. As this is written, the first Gulfhawk is in an air museum at Santee, S.C., and today bears small resemblence to its original configuration. It is registered with the FAA as a "Hawk 1A."

Another Hawk biplane in civil license was Jess Bristow's Essohawk, NX-9110, seen on the air show circuit during the late thirties. This was apparently the Curtiss company demonstrator of the Conqueror-powered P-6 which Jimmy Doolittle flew extensively for Curtiss in a quest for overseas orders.

A third P-6 in civil license for a time was NX-72K, sold to Japan and retroactively called a "Hawk I" in Curtiss records.

In June, 1930, Curtiss began work on a new compact fighter design based upon a Navy specification that anticipated operation from both carrier decks and airborne rigid dirigibles. Actually, direct mention of the dirigible requirement was avoided, but it was implicit in the aircraft size and weight limitations and in the firm demand for unobstructed pilot's vision ahead and above. The Curtiss XF9C-1 Sparrowhawk resulted, and it beat out rival designs by Fokker and Berliner-Joyce. It was accepted by the Navy for test at the end of March, 1931.

The XF9C-1 fuselage was all-metal semi-monocoque in construction with vertical and horizontal stabilizers built-in as integral parts and also metal-covered. The rudder was metal-covered; elevators fabric-covered. Wings were fabric-covered with spars of aluminum alloy tubes and ribs stamped from aluminum sheets. Flotation bags were located outboard of the interplane struts in upper wings and inflated by a carbon dioxide tank carried in a streamlined housing on the belly between the landing gear struts. Long-span Frieze-type ailerons were in top wing only. Engine was the Wright R-975C which developed 420 hp at 2,300 rpms at sea level.

Navy test pilots complained that the upper gulled wings made ground or carrier landing approaches difficult due to poor forward/

The little F9C-2 Sparrowhawk operated from the dirigibles Akron and Macon. Seven were built, plus the prototype.

downward visibility, so Curtiss built a second Sparrowhawk with company funds which, although it was registered as a civil aircraft (NX-986M) and had no Navy serial, was designated the XF9C-2. This one was painted dark blue, featured a single-strut, wire-braced landing gear and had its upper wings raised four inches to improve pilot-vision for normal landings. The XF9C-2 was completed in November, 1931, and though pilots felt that it was less than an ideal carrier fighter, it was at least "acceptable" for shipboard use — which was all that was necessary, because its primary function was to operate from the new dirigibles Akron and Macon.

In April, 1932, the Navy placed an order for six production F9C-2's with the understanding that only one would be built until final configuration was settled upon following actual airship hook-ups (the Navy had had previous air hook-up experience, since July, 1929, using the dirigible Los Angeles and Consolidated N2Y trainers and Vought OU-1's).

The first F9C-2 was delivered a month later and, after replacing the single-strut landing gear with a conventional tripod gear, plus addition of an eight-inch-wide section to the vertical fin and a three-

31

inch aluminum strip to the rudder's trailing edge for added yaw stability while on the airship trapeze, the design was firmed up and the remaining five planes delivered.

Since there has been so much confusion in the past regarding delivery of the six production and two experimental Sparrowhawks, we'll reproduce here entries taken directly from Curtiss company's bound volume, "Airplane Billing, 1/1/31 - 12/31/40," kept by the Sales & Contract Division:

XF9C-1	1 produced	$40,217.21	del. 3/31	s/n A-8731
F9C-2	1 produced	$27,356.00	del. 5/2/32	9056
F9C-2	4 produced	$23,561.00	del. 8/5/32	9058—9061
F9C-2	1 produced	24,956.00	del. 9/12/32	9057
XF9C-2	1 produced	$30,000.00	del. 1/10/33	9264

From the above, you'll note that the XF9C-2 did not become Navy property until January 10, 1933, at which time it was finally taken out of civil license and given Navy serial 9264 (the Navy dropped the "A" prefix for aircraft serials in 1932). Actually, this craft had been at Anacostia during much of the preceding year, but was returned to Curtiss (as was the XF9C-1), where it was modified into the F9C-2 configuration before final delivery to North Island on the above date. The XF9C-1 was re-delivered to Lakehurst Naval Air Station in December, 1932.

The dirigible Akron crashed during a storm off the New Jersey coast on April 4, 1933, taking the lives of 73 of the 76 men aboard, including that of Rear Admiral William Moffett who had headed the Navy's Bureau of Aeronautics since it was formed in 1921. No Sparrowhawks were carried that day.

The Macon was commissioned in June, 1933, and the six F9C-2's and the XF9C-2 were shifted to Moffett Field, Sunnyvale, California to operate from the new airship (both Akron and Macon could carry five Sparrowhawks internally, but four was the usual complement). The XF9C-1 went to the Naval Aircraft Factory at that time and was scrapped.

On February 12, 1935, the Macon crashed into the Pacific near Big Sur, California and four F9C-2's went down with the mother ship, although only two of the 81 men aboard were lost. Two of the remaining three Sparrowhawks were surveyed at San Diego in 1936, while the last one went back to Anacostia, then to the N.A.S. at Norfolk where it remained until presented to the National Air & Space Museum (Smithsonian) in 1939. It is there today. Close inspection indicates that it is probably the XF9C-2, s/n 9264.

The Navy's F11C-2 Goshawk was Cyclone-powered. After entering service, it received a modified aft turtle-deck and full canopy and was re-designated the BFC-2. Navy bought 27.
Photo: U.S. Navy

During this same period of the early thirties, the performance of the Air Corps' P-6E Hawk, and a variant of it built as a Curtiss company demonstrator, the Goshawk, captured Navy interest and a contract was let on April 16, 1932 for two Goshawks to be designated XF11C-1 and XF11C-2.

This purchase too is a bit confusing because the Navy accepted the Curtiss demonstrator as one of the two planes ordered and designated it XF11C-2, while the XF11C-1, yet to be built, was not delivered until the following September.

In any case, the XF11C-1 was an interesting machine, partly because it was equipped with a twin-row radial engine, the 600-hp experimental Wright R-1510, but mainly because it used the metal-framed (fabric-covered) wings from the Army's XP/YP-23 Hawk. These wings served well enough on the XF11C-1, which ended up as a test vehicle for NACA (forerunner of NASA), but this same metal wing structure was to prove the ruination of a later Hawk.

The XF11C-2 was powered with a Cyclone R-1820-78 engine rated at 700 hp at 1,900 rpms at 4,000 ft, and had longer landing gear struts than the dash-one, along with low pressure tires. The fact that it had been built as a company demonstrator revealed Curtiss' plans for it as an export fighter, whether or not the U.S. Navy decided to buy. And indeed, as the Hawk II, its foreign sales greatly exceeded domestic deliveries, with a total of 127 going to nine different countries.

The U.S. Navy bought 27 production F11C-2's. These craft differed from the XF11C-2 in that, for carrier operation, the Navy preferred the larger wheels and high-pressure tires of earlier Hawks, and the Townend ring on the engine had a chord about half-way between the narrow one of the XF11C-2 and the rather wide one enclosing the twin-row engine on the XF11C-1.

In March, 1933, these craft were delivered to VF-1B, the "High Hat" Squadron, then serving aboard the Saratoga. A year later, the F11C-2 Goshhawks were re-designated BFC-2's when the Navy adopted its "bomber-fighter" category. In the meantime, the rear turtle decks were raised on these planes and sliding cockpit canopies added, although the BFC-2's were often flown without these enclosures. Since Curtiss records do not show that the Navy was billed for these modifications, it's possible this work was done at the Naval Aircraft Factory.

The fourth F11C-2, s/n 9269, was converted to the XF11C-3 and delivered to the Navy May 27, 1933. It was identical to the service Goshawks except for a retractable landing gear and the forward fuselage modification that required, and had an aft turtle deck that was neither as high as that of the BFC-2 nor possessed a head rest. The Navy liked this airplane (later called the XBF2C-1), and ordered 27 production models with elevated aft turtle decks and partial canopies — plus the metal-framed wings that had proven satisfactory on the XF11C-1. The result was the BF2C-1, and ex-Curtiss engineer Edwin C. Walton explained for us the problem that immediately showed up on this one:

"Production Hawks up to the BF2C-1 had wood structure in the wings; spruce beams (spars) with plywood web, spruce ribs, and doped Flightex fabric covering. But the BF2C-1 was produced with aluminum alloy beams and ribs in the wings, and it just happened that the period of vibration of that structure coincided perfectly with the cruising rpms of the R-1820 engine (we didn't know too much about dynamic testing then), with the result that the aircraft just about shook apart in cruising speed..."

The 27 BF2C-1's therefore had a service life of about a year,

A BF2C-1 Hawk flown by Lt. Cmdr. J.D. Barner of VB-5B operating from the USS Ranger in 1935. These planes had short service life due to matching periodic vibration frequency between metal-framed wings and Cyclone engine at cruise setting.

Photo: U.S. Navy

Export Hawk II was similar to Navy's Goshawk. This one went to Turkey. Len Povey, as boss of Cuban Air Force during the thirties, proved the Hawk II an outstanding aerobatic machine. It sold for $12,980, less engine, prop and armament.

serving with VB-5 aboard the Ranger.

But the *same* airplane, fitted with the old reliable Hawk wooden wings (designed by George Page in 1924), may be considered the most successful biplane Hawk of all: It was sold to four foreign countries as the Hawk III, and a total of 138 were built, more than were constructed of any other Hawk biplane model.

Export Biplane Hawks

Biplane Hawks in small numbers went to foreign buyers beginning with the P-1A in 1926 (Japan had previously bought one PW-8), although during the twenties overseas buyers were more interested in two-place and multi-purpose craft than in fighters. The Hawk II, essentially the same as the XF11C-2 (except that it had the -53 Cyclone instead of the -78), was the first Curtiss fighter sold in the foreign market in significant numbers.

Cuba, which had bought three P-6S's (P&W Wasp-powered P-6) in 1930, purchased four Hawk II's which were inherited by the Batista Rebels who overthrew the Machado regime in 1933 in the famous "Sergeants' Revolt." Ex-sergeant Fulgencio Batista (who was to rule Cuba until he was kicked out by Fidel Castro in 1959) hired U.S. akro-pilot and ex-barnstormer Leonard Povey to run his air force, and Povey spent much of his time aerobating a stripped-down Hawk II to entertain visiting dignitaries. Povey accidentally invented the "Cuban-8" maneuver in his Cuban Hawk at the 1936 All American Air Show at Miami.

A year before, this same model Hawk had been in combat during the Gran Chaco War between Bolivia and Paraguay. Bolivia had taken delivery of nine Hawk II's between December 27, 1932 and June 26, 1934 (at prices ranging from $12,950 to $14,015 each for airframes), and these gave Bolivia air supremacy over Paraguay's French-built Potez 25 and Wilbault two-place monoplane fighter-bombers.

Hawk II's also fought in China during the mid-thirties, and Generalissimo Chiang Kai-shek's Nationalist forces had a total of 50 of this model.

Reports that "Curtiss fighters" were flown by the Loyalists during the Spanish Civil War against Hitler's Condor Legion, seem to be in error. Following a direct appeal from President Roosevelt (still contained in Curtiss files), Curtiss-Wright refused to accept orders from either side during that conflict. The "Curtiss fighters" mentioned in the Adolf Galland book, "The First and the Last"

Chinese Hawk III's at Lungwa, China, October 24, 1936. These Hawks were assembled in China by the Central Aircraft Manufacturing Corporation which was set up by Curtiss-Wright and later owned by William D. Pawley, long-time C-W export sales representative and international wheeler-dealer.

Photo: National Air & Space Museum

(Henry Holt & Co., 1954), were probably FF-1 Grummans built in Canada by the Canadian Car & Foundry Co., because 44 of these craft are known to have gone to the Loyalists, and the FF-1 did much resemble the export Hawk III.

The Hawk III saw a great deal of combat in China against the invading Japanese during the late thirties. As previously noted, this was practically the same airplane as the U.S. Navy's unsuccessful BF2C-1, except that it reverted to the earlier Hawk wooden wing structure. Former Curtiss-Wright engineer Edwin C. Walton, who had served as stress analyst on the BF2C-1 project, explained: "There was a great need for an improved Hawk for the export market, with retractable landing gear, and having by that time become project engineer on export aircraft for Curtiss, I tried going backward a bit. I used the old reliable wood wing structure, but with the airfoil section changed from Clark Y to Clark YH — meaning a slight up-sweep in the last couple of feet of chord to cut diving loads on the wing structure — substituted short stub exhaust stacks on the engine in lieu of the newer collector ring, modified the NACA cowl to suit,

Last Hawk biplane was the 250 mph Hawk IV, and the single example built went to Argentina. Engine was 750-hp Cyclone SR-1820F-53.

Photo: Peter M. Bowers Collection

and we found we had a winner; vibration gone, speed improved and cost lowered."

A number of China Hawk III's were built in China by the Central Aircraft Manufacturing Corporation. CAMCO was undoubtedly set up by Curtiss personnel (chief engineer was Curtiss hand E.A. Warren; plant manager was George Arnold), and it seems clear that CAMCO was owned by Curtiss-Wright at that time because the Hawk III's built there were billed to Chiang Kai-shek by the Aeroplane Division of C-W at Buffalo. CAMCO became the property of William D. Pawley — a high rolling wheeler-dealer who collected friends in high places, and who was officially Curtiss-Wright's export sales representative — in 1938 or thereabouts. We'll return to Mr. Pawley later.

Argentina, which had previously purchased ten Hawk III's, bought the one and only Hawk IV, which was built in 1936 and was the final biplane model. The Hawk IV used the Hawk III airframe, and differed from its predecessor in that it had a full, sliding cockpit canopy, carburetor heat and an exhaust collector ring. Curtiss advertised its top speed as 250 mph. It appears that Argentina was authorized to build the Hawk IV under license, but never did.

A complete list of all export Hawk biplanes is contained in Part 6.

NAVY, MARINE & EXPORT BIPLANE HAWKS, SPECIFICATIONS & PERFORMANCE

	F6C-3	F6C-4	F7C-1	F9C-2	F11C-2	BF2C-1	Hawk II	Hawk III
Span upper	31' 6"	31' 6"	32' 8"	25' 6"	31' 6"	31' 6"	31' 6"	31' 6"
Span lower	26'	26'	28'	23' 3"	26' 6"	26' 6"	26' 6"	26' 6"
Length	22' 5½"	22'	22' 2"	20' 2"	25'	23'	25'	23' 6"
Gross weight	2963 lbs	2785	2782	2770	4120	4555	3850	4317
Empty weight	2359 lbs	2124	2105	2089	3111	3370	2880	3213
Fuel capacity	100 gal*	100*	100*	63	94*	110*	105*	110*
Max. speed	159 mph	158	150	176	205	225	210	240
Initial climb	1950 fpm	2300	1870	1700	2150	2150	2350	2200
Stall speed	60 mph	56	52	62	63.5	69	67	67.9
Service ceiling	20,000 ft	21,900	21,500	19,200	24,000	24,000	24,000	25,800
Range	380 mi	320	315	252	560†	570†	570†	575†
Engine	V-1150	R-1340	R-1340B	R-975E-3	R-1820-78	R-1820-04	R-1820F-3	R-1820F-53 or SR-1820F-53

* Internal and external total.
† With external tank.

The first Hawk 75, pictured May 27, 1935, originally fitted with experimental twin-row radial, the Wright R-1670.

Photo: Donovan R. Berlin

PART 3: THE HAWK 75 AND P-36

In September, 1934, Ralph S. Damon, who had succeeded Clement M. Keys as president of the Curtiss-Wright Corporation, learned that engineer Donovan R. Berlin had left Northrop and, aware of Berlin's reputation, offered him a job.

Damon (later president of American Air Lines) made a good choice. Berlin had entered aviation in 1921 when, a few days after graduation from Purdue University, he began as wind tunnel operator at the Army's McCook Field. Berlin joined Donald Douglas in 1926, advanced to chief production design engineer within three years, then quit to go with Northrop. There, Don helped bring forth a series of advanced airplanes, the Alpha, Beta, Gamma series, pioneering in stressed-skin construction, and was Northrop's chief engineer when he was fired in June, 1934, after refusing to accept a new wing design Berlin believed would be subject to flutter.

Berlin arrived in Buffalo on the 21st of October and immediately started to work on the project the company called "Design 75."* Speed was necessary because this airplane was intended for a fighter competition scheduled at Wright Field on May 27, 1935.

---

*Curtiss-Wright model numbers — that is, an attempt at a consistent model-number system — began with the Model 75, and all previous C-W aircraft were retroactively numbered (the P-1, for example became the Model 34). But this system held small significance for previous Hawks because most of them no longer existed by this time, and because too many early Curtiss designs were skipped altogether. Late in WW-II, even some of the Model H87 Warhawks apparently failed to receive suffix letters to identify variants.

"The Army specs indicated in broad terms what the Air Corps hoped to get in the way of a new fighter," Berlin says. "Principally, this meant all-metal, low-wing and a speed of 300 mph. I worked out the design, using the engine then available to me, the experimental Wright R-1670 of 900-hp, a twin-row radial that turned out to be a clunker.

"Our prototype Hawk 75, with civil registration NX-17Y, first flew in mid-April, 1935, and performed very well. We had a little trouble with the brakes, and I added a small amount of rudder area to give improved yaw control near the stall. Otherwise, the airframe was right as originally laid out."

None of the fighters, including a Seversky and a Northrop, was ready for the tests at Wright Field in May, so the Air Corps postponed the competition until August — at which time, with all competitors still having their troubles, the trials were again put off and re-scheduled for April, 1936.

Meanwhile, the Hawk 75 had shed its R-1670 in favor of an experimental P&W Twin Wasp Jr, the R-1535, but that engine too was a failure (P&W later abandoned it), so Berlin put a new Wright R-1820 single-row Cyclone in the Hawk for the 1936 competition.

Now, the F Model Cyclone had appeared in 1932, rated at 750 hp. Output had been increased to 875 hp by 1936, but this version of the R-1820 had not been sufficiently de-bugged at the time and, with the engine delivering only 75% power, the Hawk 75 lost out to the Seversky in the spring of 1936. The Army ordered 77 production P-35 Severskys.

The Air Corps did, however, give C-W a "consolation prize," as Berlin puts it; an order for three service test models of the Hawk, designated Y1P-36's, and asked that these planes be fitted with the new P&W R-1830 Twin Wasp engine.

"That engine proved the best to date for us," Berlin says, "and we took a Y1P-36 to the fighter competition at Wright Field in May, 1937, and won. In fact, the Air Corps liked the airplane so well it bought 210 on June 6, 1937, the largest U.S. fighter plane order since WW-I. And concurrent with that sale, we also produced 200 Hawk 75's for the French. Our research and development costs on that airplane, by the way, totaled about $750,000, which included 27,000 man-hours invested in the engineering."

Delivery of the Air Corps' production order began in April, 1938, with 177 aircraft built as P-36A's, one became a P-36B, fitted with the R-1830-25 engine of 1,100 hp; one became the XP-40, another the

The Army Air Corps ordered three service test models of the Hawk 75, specified that they be fitted with R-1830 Twin Wasps, and designated these machines Y1P-36's.

Photo: Donovan R. Berlin

Though wearing Air Corps paint job, the H75-R was a company-owned ship (NX-22028), fitted with P&W R-1830-19 (SC2-G) and turbo supercharger.

Photo: USAF

The XP-42 (H75-S) Hawk was an experiment in tightly cowling the air-cooled R-1830-31 Twin Wasp to reduce drag. Tested between March, 1939 and May, 1941, it eventually a-chieved 343 mph, but created more problems than it solved.

Photo: Tom Ellis

XP-42, and the last 30 were designated P-36C's when a .30 caliber gun was installed in each wing (in addition to the pair of sychronized guns atop the cowl), after this four-gun set up was proven with s/n 38-085, making it a P-36C.

The only external differences of significance between the P-36A's and Y1P-36's were addition of adjustable knob-like fairings around the nose-cowl gun ports and cowl flaps on the production craft. A number of P-36A's were temporarily taken out of service and used at various times to try different armament combinations. In September, 1939, the 174th P-36A became the XP-36D when fitted with two .50 caliber guns in the nose and a pair of .30 calibers in each wing. The 147th P-36A similarly became the XP-36E when it received new outer wing panels containing four .30 caliber guns in each wing; while the 172nd craft was re-designated XP-36F with installation of a 23-mm Madsen cannon on the underside of each wing plus the two nose guns (one .30 and one .50 caliber). Meanwhile, the first Y1P-36 was flown with a four-bladed prop, and later with co-axial props, while the 180th production craft was equipped with streamlined skis and a fixed landing gear for a time.

In addition to the Model 75 prototype, NX-17Y, a second com-pany-owned 75 was built and had civil registration NX-22028. This craft, fitted with a turbo supercharger, was tested at Wright Field wearing Air Corps markings (without numbers) and was designated

44

the H75-R. Its supercharger was located behind the engine in the bottom of the forward fuselage, with the inter-cooler in a streamlined housing farther aft on the belly. But its R-1830-19 Twin Wasp had an unsolved bearing problem at high operating temperatures and, anyway, turbo supercharging was still impractical for fighter aircraft at that time, awaiting in particular perfection of automatic control. Therefore, the H75-R Hawk was eventually returned to Curtiss and was sold to a civilian buyer after the war.

During the time the P-36's were delivered, the Air Corps had six Pursuit Groups (1st, 8th, 15th, 16th, 18th and 20th), and all but the 15th received at least one squadron of the new Hawks. However, in February, 1940, the Air Corps began an expansion program that resulted in a total of 25 Pursuit Groups* by October 1, 1941, and the 200 or so P-36's were spread thinner to see service with such new units as the 35th, 51st and 56th Pursuit Groups — although by that time P-40's had entered the Air Corps' inventory in some numbers and the P-36 was no longer regarded as a first-line fighter aircraft.

When the Japanese launched their surprise attack on Pearl Harbor, Sunday, December 7, 1941, at least four P-36A's of the 46th Pursuit Squadron, 15th Pursuit Group, escaped damage on the ground during the initial strike at Wheeler Field and managed to get into the air; and at Haleiwa, a gunnery strip on northern Oahu, another P-36A of the 47th Squadron joined the brief battle (described in Part 4).

The P-36 Hawk saw only that single, desperate hour of combat in the hands of Americans — but it had, more than two years before, already secured a proud listing in the annals of aerial warfare. As the Hawk 75 (H75 *Chasse* 1) with France's Armee d l'Air, it was the sharpest edge of the French defensive sword from the beginning of WW-II in September, 1939, until France fell ten months later.

*These were, in addition to the six older Groups, the 14th, 24th, 31st, 32nd, 33rd, 34th, 35th, 36th, 37th, 49th, 50th, 51st, 52nd, 53rd, 54th, 55th, 56th, 57th and 58th. Two years later, the USAAF had a total of 74 Fighter Groups, not counting the 16th, deactivated in October, 1943. All Pursuit Groups were re-designated "Fighter Groups" in May, 1942.
During WW-II, a USAAF fighter group consisted of — on paper, at least — 111 to 126 aircraft; 183 officers and 811 enlisted men. Normally, each group was made up of three Squadrons of 27 to 36 planes each plus reserves.
British Commonwealth squadrons were approximately 12 aircraft each; Luftwaffe *staffeln* operated nine aircraft each; and the Italian Regia Aeronautica *squadriglie* were also composed of nine planes each.
A French *groupe de chasse* consisted of 18 to 24 fighter planes divided into two *escadrilles* of nine to 12 planes each.

Hawk P-36A of the 55th Pursuit Squadron, 20th Pursuit Group which was stationed at Barksdale Field, La., although photo apparently taken elsewhere, probably March Field, Calf.

Photo: Merle C. Olmsted Collection

A P-36C photographed March 25, 1942. Both group number and squadron insignia painted out with solid olive-drab over-all. Thus we know only that this was s/n 38-191, airplane number 22 within whatever squadron and group it belonged to.

Photo: National Archives

Argentina H75-0 Hawk; Cyclone-powered, .30 caliber gun in each wing along with external bomb racks. This one wears Argentina's blue-and-white roundels and Sun of May emblem on rudder, along with temporary U.S. civil registration. May 11, 1937.

Photo: Donovan R. Berlin

France bought 100 Hawk 75's in May, 1938, and deliveries began late that year. These machines were essentially the same as the U.S. Air Corps' P-36A's and were fitted with the P&W R-1830-SC3G Twin Wasp, rated at 1,050 hp at 2,700 rpms at 7,000 feet burning 87 octane fuel. These craft were assembled at Bourges under the direction of C-W test pilot Gerrardus B. "Jerry" Clark.

"Once the engine problems were solved with the Hawk 75, we had a real airplane," Clark says. "This airplane wasn't as fast as, say, the Me 109; but as a fighter pilot, I thought its handling characteristics were terrific: short turning radius, spun well, recovered well, good rate-of-roll; an excellent gun platform.

"By the time the war started the following September, four French units — *Groupes de Chasse* I/4, I/5, II/4 and II/5 — were equipped with the Hawk; and despite all this latter-day talk about the Me 109E's superiority over the Hawk 75 in combat, those French pilots were clearly unaware of any such 'disadvantage,' and their records are there to prove it. French Hawk pilots officially destroyed 311 enemy aircraft for a loss of 29 of their own killed. Near the end, the odds ran at least six-to-one against them in the air."

Luftwaffe aircraft recognition poster of 1939 pictured a pair of French H75-A1's (above), and prototype Hawk NX-17Y fitted with it's third engine, the R-1820-G3 Cyclone. Poster warned German pilots of the H75's armor behind pilot.

Photo: U.S. Navy

Clark estimates that the French never had more than 175 Hawks in action, and that is close. France ordered a second 100 (H75-A2; two additional guns) which were shipped between May 16th and July 29th, 1939. Then, an order was placed for 135 H75-A3's (same as A2 but with more powerful S1C3G engine), and finally ordered 395 H75-A4's powered with the Wright Cyclone GR-1820G engine. Between 55 and 60 of the A3's reached France or were re-routed to Casablanca in French Morocco. Six A4's got to France before the French-German Armistice, and 23 A4's were diverted to Martinique (where they remained for 2½ years until released to Free French forces after the invasion of North Africa by the Allies). Since four H75-A2's were lost at sea, the French could hardly have had more than 200-225 Hawk 75's in France, not counting losses (194 A1's and A2's; six A4's and perhaps 20-25 A3's).

The British accepted the undelivered A3's, which the Royal Air Force (RAF) called "Mohawk III's," as well as 225 French A4's, called "Mohawk IV's" in RAF service (only 284 planes of the 395-plane order for A4's were actually built).

After an eight-month "Phoney War" period through the winter of 1939-1940, the Battle of France (Hilter called it "Operation Yellow") began May 10, 1940, and raged until France gave up on June 25th. And though the defeated French were left with little enough to be proud of, the Hawk *groupes* in the Armee d l'Air fought fiercely, accounting for one-third of all French air victories. Near the end, a fifth Hawk *groupe,* III/2, went into action, and though it fought but eleven days, it shot down 17 of the enemy for a loss of two of its pilots.

But the Germans entered Paris on the 14th, and on the 17th of May, 1940, French Premier Petain began seeking an armistice with Germany while the remaining British started evacuating to England. During the next week, ten of the remaining fighter units in France, including all Hawk *groupes,* flew across the Mediterranean to North Africa. After the French surrender, the puppet Vichy Government was theoretically neutral, and the Hawks at Casablanca and Senegal spent the next two years on peaceful patrols.

Then, the Allied invasion of North Africa in November, 1942 added a tragic and pointless page to the brave history of the French Hawk *groupes. Groupes* I/5 at Rabat, and II/5 at Casablanca were in the U.S. landing sector and tangled with U. S. Navy F4F Wildcats from Task Force 34. In two great air battles on November 8th, a total of 14 Hawks and eight Wildcats went down. Most of the remaining Hawks were so badly shot up they never fought again; and within three days all French forces in North Africa — reluctant from the beginning to fight against Americans for their Nazi masters — put aside their weapons. The survivors of the Hawk *groupes,* soon re-equipped with P-40's and P-47's, fought the rest of the war on the side of the Allies.

Hawk 75 M's and N's (fixed-gear versions) also saw combat. Thailand's H75-N's fought briefly as that country was overrun by the Japanese in December, 1941; and China's Air Force, under Chennault, had three squadrons of Hawk 75-M's in 1938-1939 which fought the Japanese prior to WW-II. And twenty H75-A7's (Twin Wasp; retractable gear) of the Royal Netherlands East Indies Air Force offered stiff resistance to the Japanese from Bandoeng, Java, early in WW-II until that Dutch possession fell to the Nipponese invader.

HAWK 75 & P-36 ENGINES

P&W Twin Wasp	**Rating**	**RPMS**	**Man. Press.**	**Altitude**
R-1830-17	1200 hp	2700		take-off
	1050	2550		6,500 ft
(P-36A/P-36C)				
	Fuel	**Bore/Stroke**	**Comp. ratio**	**Weight**
	100	5.5 X 5.5	6.7:1	1,403 lbs

P&W Twin Wasp	**Rating**	**RPMS**	**Man. Press.**	**Altitude**
R-1830-S1C3G	1200 hp	2700	48. Hg	take-off
	1050	2550	41.	7,500 ft
(H75-A3 & A6)				
	Fuel	**Bore/Stroke**	**Comp. ratio**	**Weight**
	91/98	5.5 X 5.5	6.7:1	1,467 lbs

Wright Cyclone	**Rating**	**RPMS**	**Man. Press.**	**Altitude**
GR-1820-G3	875 hp	2200	38.5 Hg	take-off
	840	2100	35.	8,700 ft
(H75-M, N and				
O, fixed-gear)	**Fuel**	**Bore/Stroke**	**Comp. ratio**	**Weight**
	87	6.125 X 6.875	6.45:1	1,198 lbs

Wright Cyclone	**Rating**	**RPMS**	**Man. Press.**	**Altitude**
R-1820-G205A	1200 hp	2500	44. Hg	take-off
	1100	2500	40.	5,100 ft
(H75-A4, A8 & A9)				
	Fuel	**Bore/Stroke**	**Comp. ratio**	**Weight**
	91/96	6.125 X 6.875	6.5:1	1,300 lbs

	Y1P-36	P-36A	H75-M	H75-A3
Wing span	37′ 3½″	37′ 3½″	37′ 4″	37′ 4″
Wing area	236 sq ft	236	236	236
Length	27′ 10½″	28′ 6″	28′ 7″	28′ 7″
Gross weight	5,418 lbs	5,470	5,305	5,692
Empty weight	4,506 lbs	4,567	3,975	4,483
Maximum speed	300 mph*	313*	280*	311*
Landing speed	69.2 mph	69	64	69
Initial climb	2100 fpm	2600	2340	2350
Service ceiling	33,200 ft	33,700	31,800	33,700
Range, normal	885 mi	825	547	820
Landing gear	retract	retract	fixed	retract
Engine	R-1830-13	R-1830-17	GR-1820-G3	R-1830-S1C3G

*at 10,000 ft

The Air Corps bought thirteen YP-37's for service test. Engine was a supercharged Allison V-1710-21. Unreliability of supercharger and success of the XP-40 were main factors that doomed this Hawk design.

Photo: Air Force Museum

PART 4: Y1P-37; P-40 SERIES; TOMAHAWKS, KITTYHAWKS & WARHAWKS

U.S. Army Air Corps/Air Forces

Early in 1937, Curtiss-Wright realized that the P-36, as good as it was for its time, would soon be surpassed. "We needed something out ahead," as Donovan Berlin put it. And since the Army still had faith in liquid-cooled aircraft engines — especially for fighters — and had put a lot of development money into the Allison V-1710, Berlin and his small engineering force began re-working a P-36 airframe to take the twelve-cylinder Allison.

The first airplane to result from this concept was the XP-37 (Design 75I), built specifically to house the V-1710-11 Allison with a General Electric turbo supercharger. This craft was longer than the P-36, with the cockpit moved far aft and faired into the vertical tail. The turbo unit, radiator and inter-cooler were encased within the fuselage between the pilot and the engine. The XP-37 was completed by April 1, 1937, but damaged during delivery and then re-delivered June 16, 1937. The Air Corps apparently felt it had promise, because thirteen service test models were ordered the following December.

The thirteen Y1P-37's were powered with the improved V-1710-21 Allison and had longer noses, modified radiators and cockpits moved somewhat forward. But even with expert mixture-control handling, this craft barely achieved 340 mph, and the supercharger

The XP-40 originally flew with a belly radiator not greatly different to that of the later P-51. The radiator was moved forward within the engine nacelle where it shared a small air scoop with the oil cooler (above). This proved inadequate and the scoop was slightly enlarged for the fighter competition at Wright Field in January, 1939. The XP-40 easily won, and its radiator scoop was again enlarged for the first production P-40's.

Photo: Donovan R. Berlin

unit, relatively undeveloped, had regulator problems and a penchant for throwing buckets from the turbine wheel.

It was clear to Berlin that Curtiss-Wright did not have the time to develop a turbo supercharger system for the Allison (after all, GE engineers had been working on such units since 1918 at McCook and Wright Fields. If they hadn't yet found all the answers, it was unrealistic to expect a quantum advance from C-W or Allison engine people).* Therefore, Berlin approached the problem from a different angle.

"In the urgency of the times," Berlin says, "I talked the Allison Division of General Motors into giving me an estimate of the altitude power which could be obtained with their engine·if they were to increase the rpms of the internal diffuser (blower). The answer came out

*Practical and reliable turbo superchargers did not appear for U.S. warplanes until 1942; which is a principal reason the P-38 Lightning — also begun in 1937 — was late entering service.

at 1,050 hp at 10,000 feet. Inasmuch as Air Corps specs at that time called for performance at 10,000, this was great. So, I made an estimate of what this engine installation would do for a P-36, submitted it to Wright Field on March 3, 1938, and got immediate approval."

This airplane was designated XP-40, and it was put together from the tenth P-36A (s/n 38-010) airframe and an Allison V-1710-19 engine rated at 1,160 hp. The AC order was officially approved in July, 1938, and the XP-40 made its first flight October 14, 1938. It had one .30 and one .50 caliber gun atop the cowl with the carburetor intake in between. A small oil cooler nestled beneath the nose, and the radiator was in a scoop on the belly behind the wing's trailing edge. Maximum speed was 342 mph at 12,200 feet — although Berlin promised General Arnold 365 mph as soon as the new V-1710-33 engine was ready and a few minor changes made.

A fighter competition was flown at Wright Field, January 25,

Production P-40 further enlarged air scoop, had short exhaust stacks and gave up P-36 wheel fairings in place of clam-shell doors to cover landing gear struts.

Photo: Donovan R. Berlin

55

1939 and the XP-40 — which had its radiator moved to beneath the nose by then at the instigation of Curtiss' Sales & Contract Division — won over the XP-38, XP-39 and Seversky AP-4 (as well as the XP-37 and Hawk 75R), and this resulted in a Air Corps order, dated April 26, 1939, for 524 production P-40's at a cost of $12,872,898.

Before production could start, the design needed the modifications Berlin had listed. The change to the Allison V-1710-33 required more radiator area, and the larger scoop also housed the oil cooler. Cooling gills were added, and the original straight exhausts were replaced by six individual stacks on each side. The P-36 wheel-fairings were discarded.

Only 199 units of the 524-plane order were actually built as P-40's. One was converted to the P-40G on the production line when given H81-A2 Tomahawk wings containing two guns in each panel (in addition to the pair of fuselage guns). The next 131 were delivered early in 1941 as P-40B's, which were the same as H81-A2 Tomahawks; and the last 193 units, delivered in April and May, 1941, were P-40C's, similar to the B's except fittings were provided for a 52-gal belly tank, internal self-sealing fuel tanks were re-designed and improved radios were installed. Later, another 44 of the original P-40's were converted to P-40G's with Tomahawk wings and armor plate; and one, s/n 40-326, became (unofficially) a P-40A when converted for photo work.

The first three P-40's were used for service test, though were never officially given the "YP" designation. The 8th PG at Langley Field was the first to be equipped with P-40's in September, 1940. The 20th PG at March Field got the next batch, and then the 31st PG at Selfridge began receiving its P-40 Hawks.

By the end of April, 1941, the 15th and 18th Pursuit Groups at Wheeler Field, Hawaii, had received a total of 55 of the 131 P-40B's, with an additional 31 going to the 24th PG stationed at Clark Field in the Philippines. On December 7th, 1941, when America was plunged into WW-II, the 15th PG and 18th PG in Hawaii had 87 P-40B's and 12 P-40C's. By that time, the 24th PG in the Philippines could count 107 P-40B's and E's in the 3rd, 17th, 20th and 21st Pursuit Squadrons — although it appears that no more than 18 of the 31 P-40B's were operational due to lack of parts, and some of the P-40E's were still uncrated.

Meanwhile, a total of 70 P-40B's and C's went to the 16th PG in Panama, while the 35th Squadron of the 36th PG went to Puerto Rico (March, 1941) with P-40B's; and on August 6th, 1941, the 33rd Squadron of the 8th PG arrived in Iceland equipped with 30 P-40C's.

P-40G's resulted when 45 P-40's were given Tomahawk wings with two .30 caliber guns in each panel in addition to the standard nose armament. H81-A2 wing panels also contained self-sealing fuel tanks.

Photo: Merle C. Olmsted Collection

Early Pacific Fighting

When war came in the Pacific, the only working radar on Oahu — a crude early set — picked up the incoming Japanese first wave of 183 planes when the enemy was still 130 miles away, but the enlisted operator's report was discounted by the lieutenant who received the telephoned alert at 07:04 hours. Nineteen minutes before that, the first shot had been fired by the U.S. Destroyer Ward when she spotted the periscope of a Japanese midget submarine in restricted waters just outside Pearl Harbor. The Ward attacked with gunfire and depth charges, reporting the action to Pearl Harbor. This incident, too, had failed to arouse the great American base.

No alarm was ever sounded. At the Army's Wheeler and Hickam Fields, the Marine airfield at Ewa and the Navy installations at Kaneohe and Ford Island, war came suddenly, at 07:55 hours, when the first enemy bombs began to fall. The enemy's initial attack knocked out 72 airplanes (62 P-40B's) at Wheeler on the ground, and killed 32 airmen. Of the twelve P-40C's at Bellows belonging to the 44th Pursuit Squadron, three were shot down during take-off or within seconds afterwards, and nine destroyed on the ground.

Four P-40C's and a P-36A Hawk got into the air from Haleiwa, where the 47th Squadron had gone for gunnery practice. These were flown by Lts. Kenneth Taylor, George Welch, John Webster, John

A P-40B at factory, February 25, 1941. Price for airframe was $33,429.71. Engine, prop instruments, radio, armament, brought complete delivered price to $60,562. Late in the war, P-40N's were delivered, complete, for $44,892.

The men behind the P-36/P-40 program. Seated, Air Corps representative Maj. A.E. Simonin (L) and C-W General Manager Burdette S. Wright. Standing (L to R), J.A. Williams, Wright's assistant; Donovan R. Berlin, Chief Engineer and designer of the P-36/P-40; Sales Manager William Crosswell and Factory Manager P.N. Jansen.

Daines and Robert Rogers. But by the time they reached the scene of the action, the Japanese first strike was gone, so this flight landed at Wheeler to refuel. Before they could get airborne again the enemy's second wave of 130 planes arrived. Rogers, Welch, Taylor and Brown got off in P-40C's; John Daines settled for a P-36A — and was shot down by American anti-aircraft fire.

Both Taylor and Welch accounted for two enemy aircraft as the P-40's were joined by four more P-36A's flown by Lts. Gordon Sterling, Lewis Sanders, J.M. Thacker and P. Rasmussen. The P-36 Hawks attacked a formation of B5N1 Kates, and Sterling went down as Sanders and Rasmussen each flamed a Kate. After once again refueling and re-arming, Welch got two more of the enemy to bring his total to four, and Harry Brown got one. Taylor took a bullet in the arm but landed safely. No Navy or Marine planes got into the air from Kaneohe or Ewa.

Shortly after 10:00 hours, the attack was over. The Japanese, employing 423 aircraft (373 combat types), had sunk or damaged 18 American warships, destroyed 188 U.S. warplanes and damaged 159 (25 P-40B's, two P-40C's and 16 P-36A's were still flyable). The enemy's sneak attack* left behind 2,467 American dead (2,086 Navy officers and men) and more than 1,500 wounded. Cost to Japan was 29 airplanes and 55 men.

Almost simultaneously with the Pearl Harbor strike, the Japanese hit British Malaya, Thailand (where, for a few desperate hours, Hawk III's and Hawk 75's of Thailand's Air Force met the Nipponese in air combat), Singapore, Hong Kong, Guam, Midway and Wake Island. Ten and a-half hours after the Pearl Harbor attack, 108 Japanese bombers, accompanied by 84 Zeros, struck at Clark Field in the Philippines from bases on Formosa.

The raid on Clark Field came at 12:20 hours and caught most of the planes on the ground (some B-17's were just landing), despite the fact that Admiral Hart, in command of the miniscule U.S. Asiatic

---

*This term, widely used at the time, is accurate. The Japanese made no prior declaration of war, and the diplomatic note sent to the U.S. Government which, in effect, was a final ultimatum, was not delivered until 1:45 PM (13:45 hours) Washington time. By then, it was 8:15 (08:15 hours) in Hawaii and bombs were falling on Pearl Harbor. Actually, the U.S. had broken the Japenese diplomatic code and therefore knew what the note contained perhaps two hours before it was delivered. It was regarded in Washington as the last step before war could be expected. And though a special warning was sent to the Army and Navy commanders in Hawaii at that time, it was still in possession of a messenger, leisurely bicycling through the streets of Honolulu, when the attack came.

Fleet, had intercepted a Honolulu broadcast describing the disaster at Pearl Harbor at 03:00 hours* that morning and had alerted the headquarters of Gen. Douglas MacArthur.

As early as 04:00 hours that morning (an hour after receiving Admiral Hart's warning and about the time the attack ended at Pearl Harbor), P-40E's of the 3rd Pursuit Squadron took off to check a radar report of unidentified aircraft in the Manila area. They were followed by the 17th from Nichols Field and the 20th from Clark Field; but no contact with the enemy was made. Fragmentary reports of e.a. sightings came in throughout the morning and, indeed, at 09:30 hours 25 Japanese planes attacked Army installations in central and northeastern Luzon. But communications were bad — there was some sabotage — and no clear, consistent instructions came from MacArthur's Headquarters to U.S. air commanders until after the enemy had destroyed roughly half of the Far East Air Force that day.†

The noon attack on Clark Field destroyed 15 of the 17 B-17's there, and ten P-40E's (along with about 25 miscellaneous aircraft, mostly observation types). Only three pilots of the 20th Pursuit Squadron managed to get into the air, Lts. Joseph Moore, R.B. Keator and E.B. Gilmore. Four others were hit attempting to take-off. Keator got one of the enemy; Moore got two.

Twenty minutes later, the 3rd Pursuit Squadron, returning to Iba Field (about 40 miles across the mountains from Clark) were caught by Japanese planes as the P-40's attempted to land, almost out of fuel. Five Hawks were shot down and three crash-landed with empty tanks — but Lt. I.B. "Jack" Donalson, apparently flying on fumes alone, flamed down two of the enemy before his engine quit. When the Japanese left, however, only two of the 3rd's P-40E's remained.

*08:30 hours, December 7th in Hawaii; about ½ hour after the first wave of enemy planes struck Pearl Harbor. It was then 03:00 hours, December 8th in Manila, which was 5½ hours earlier than Honolulu on the clock; and one calendar day later because of the International Date Line.

†General Lewis Brereton, who had taken command of the FEAF just the day before, was at MacArthur's headquarters as early as 05:00 hours seeking permission to mount a preventative air strike against the Japanese on Formosa. He was told by General Southerland, MacArthur's chief of staff, that U.S. aircraft should not fire until they were fired upon. This incredible order may or may not have been changed before noon; statements by those involved do not agree. But the fact that such an order was given reflects the confusion in MacArthur's headquarters at that time — two hours after the news from Pearl Harbor reached the Philippines.

Nichols and Del Carmen Fields were raided the following day; and the Navy base at Cavite was wiped out on the 10th as Japanese troops began landing in northern Luzon. Although American and Filipino pilots of the FEAF continued to oppose the invader with the planes left to them (the Filipinos were flying obsolete Boeing P-26's), by the 15th of December the FEAF consisted of six B-17's and one B-18 stationed at Del Monte (about 500 miles south of Manila on Mindanao); 16 flyable P-40's (both B's and E's), seven Seversky P-35's and five O-52 and O-47 observation craft operating from Clark Field and several auxiliary grass strips — plus the handful of P-26's flown by the Philippine Air Force.

Then, on December 21, the main Japanese invasion force landed in Lingayen Gulf for its march on Manila, and General Brereton sent his remaining B-17's to Australia. Brereton was ordered to leave on the 24th, as General MacArthur and his deputy, Major General Jonathan Wainwright, retreated with their men to the Island of Corregidor in Manila Bay and the Bataan Peninsula which enclosed the bay on the west. U.S. and Filipino airmen without planes took up rifles and joined their fellow fighting men backed up on Bataan.

The remaining American fighter planes continued to fight from improvised strips on Bataan Peninsula until the day before Bataan fell, April 9, 1942. A single P-40 was all that was left by then (salvaged from the wrecks of three others) and it prompted a bitter letter, written by half-starved crew chief Sgt. Alfred Fernandez. "Dear President Roosevelt," it read, "Please send another P-40 to the Army Air Forces fighting on Bataan. The one we have is full of holes. Thank you."*

The official records (now at Maxwell AFB, Ala.) for those desperate days in the Philippines, are incomplete; but the files that do exist reveal that the P-40 pilots of the FEAF destroyed 103 enemy aircraft between December 8, 1941 and April 8, 1942. Some of the most inspiring acts of these men, especially near the end, will remain untold. Neither they nor their reports (if they bothered to write them) survived.

The Flying Tigers

In the meantime, General Claire Chennault had unleashed his Flying Tigers over Burma and China. The Tigers, officially the American Volunteer Group (AVG), are difficult to describe in few words. In

*Summon the Stars, by the same authors, A.S. Barnes & Co., New York & London, 1970.

Flying Tigers' H81-A2 Hawk mounted four .30 cal wing guns plus two fifties in nose. Plane No. 68 above was flown by Charles H. "Chuck" Older of the "Hell Angels" Squadron.

Photo: Tom Haywood

a sense, they were mercenaries — American citizens flying Chinese Air Force planes for pay. And although $600 per month for pilots and $750 for squadron leaders was at least twice as much as an Air Corps lieutenant was drawing in 1941, the Tigers themselves will tell you they didn't sign up for the money, but 1) for the adventure, 2) to fight for a cause in which they believed, and 3) because they were convinced that America would soon be drawn into war with Japan in any case. Whatever their individual reasons for joining the AVG, one fact is indisputable: Claire Lee Chennault molded them into one of the most deadly groups of fighter pilots ever assembled.

True, they were often poorly disciplined, shaved only if they felt like it, sometimes wore cowboy boots and gun-belts with revolvers, but they were, nevertheless, top professional pilots from the U.S. Air Corps, Navy, Marines and civilian test-pilots jobs when Papa Tiger recruited them via William Pawley's Central Aircraft Manufacturing Corporation. Chennault didn't teach them to fly; he taught them how to fight — in P-40's, or, more accurately, in the H81-A2 Tomahawk, the export version of the P-40B.

Chennault, a former U.S. Air Corps captain, retired in 1937 because of impaired hearing, had been hired by Generalissimo Chiang Kai-shek to run the Chinese Air Force, and Chennault returned to the U.S. early in 1941 with a reported $8.9 million with which to buy airplanes. While Pawley's people were hiring pilots and mechanics for the AVG, Chennault obtained permission to buy, and priority for delivery of the aircraft he sought; and 100 Curtiss H81-A2 Tomahawks, originally scheduled for Great Britain, were purchased and shipped via the Pawley-controlled Intercontinent Corporation from New York to Toungoo, Burma, arriving there in several ships between May 15th and December 1, 1941. The first pilots and mechanics reached there near the end of July.

Throughout that summer and fall, Chennault worked with his pilots, teaching his brand of fighter tactics and weeding out those who failed to measure up. By the time America was thrust into the war on December 7th, the Tigers were ready. Chennault divided the AVG into three squadrons (though all were understrength by American standards because, at no time during the Tigers' existence did they have more than 55 flyable airplanes): The 1st, "Adam and Eve," led by Robert Sandell; the 2nd, "Panda Bears," with Jack Newkirk as leader, and the 3rd, "Hells Angels," with Arvid Olson leading.

Three AVG pilots made a daring reconnaissance flight to photograph Japanese air strength on the 10th, but the first air battle came ten days later when the enemy sent ten bombers against Kunming where the 1st and 2nd AVG Squadrons were stationed. The Tigers shot down six bombers, crippled three which crashed on the way home and allowed one to get away. No Tigers were hit. Chennault gave his men a few words of praise, then added, "Next time, get them all."

During the following six months — until the AVG was disbanded and the USAAF 23rd Fighter Group born in its place — the Flying Tigers didn't always "get them all," but they certainly got far more than their share. During the first week — December 20-27 — the AVG blasted 55 enemy aircraft out of the skies while losing two pilots and five Tomahawks. After the first ten weeks, they could count 217 Japanese planes destroyed and 43 probables at a cost of 16 Tomahawks and the loss of four Tigers killed in combat, one killed while strafing and one a POW after bailing out over Japanese-held territory. At the end of the AVG's brief existence, it could list no less than 39 aces, ten of whom were at least double-aces.*

*One of these was Charles H. "Chuck" Older, credited with 10½ victories with the AVG and an additional eight later in the war as a USAAF pilot. Older was in the news again in 1969-1970 as the judge presiding at the sensational Sharon Tate murder trial in California.

By mid-March the AVG was down to about 20 well-used Tomahawks when it was discovered that some brand new P-40E's, intended for the Philippines, were in Accra, Africa. Since it was too late to get them to the doomed FEAF, six pilots from the 3rd AVG Squadron somehow managed to get to Accra, take possession of the Hawks, and then fly them 6,000 miles back to Kunming. More E's arrived the following month and the AVG then possessed 36 flyable fighters (These P-40E's, a few of which apparently came from the RAF, account for the fact that some have identified AVG planes as H81-A3's. The E's with the AVG had three-digit fuselage numbers).

On April 9th, 1942, Chennault was ordered back to active duty with the USAAF and, nine days later, became a brigadier general as "dissolve day" for the AVG was set at July 4th.

Meanwhile, the Tigers had retreated to Loiwing, then to Yunnanyi and Paoshan as Japanese ground forces continued to advance southwestward in China and north from Rangoon in Burma. The AVG did not stop Japan's war machine in their part of the world, but they seriously slowed it (as did the stubborn, abandoned little FEAF in the Philippines), and bought six months of precious time for the Allied fighting men who took up the Tigers' arms and continued the fight. In slightly over six months, the AVG, officially 87 pilots* strong, destroyed 286 enemy planes in the air, 240 on the ground, while significantly hurting the invader with strafing attacks on his troops and bombing (with homemade bomb racks) of his coastal shipping. Altogether, four Tigers were lost in air combat; six died strafing enemy ground targets; three were killed in training accidents; three died from enemy bombing of AVG airstrips, and three were captured by the Japanese after bailing out of crippled Tomahawks.

CBI & Pacific, 1942-1945

A patch-work outfit called the China Air Task Force (CATF), nebulously attached to the 10th Air Force which had headquarters in New Delhi, fell heir to the AVG's responsibilities, which ranged over a front 2,000 miles long over China and Burma. The CATF, commanded by General Chennault, began with the 23rd Fighter Group, made up at first of the 74th, 75th and 76th Fighter Squadrons. A little later, Chennault enticed the 16th Squadron of the 51st FG to tem-

---

*Before Pearl Harbor, twelve pilots and six crewmen were discharged out of the original 109 pilots and 150+ crewmen. During the six months of combat, ten more pilots and 37 ground personnel were "dishonorably discharged" by tough old Papa Tiger Chennault.

This P-40D (s/n 40-589), "Eva Mae," simply over-shot the runway at Shemya in the Aleutians, Oct. 23, 1944; 344th Fighter Squadron.

Photo: N.E. Taylor Collection, Air Force Museum

porarily join the 23rd for some "experience," then he never allowed the 16th to leave. The original three squadrons, which started with 51 war-weary AVG planes (31 Tomahawks; 20 P-40E's, only 20 flyable altogether) was built around a handful of ex-AVG aces and a dozen or so pilots green to combat.

In September, 1942, these four squadrons had 38 pilots and 34 flyable P-40E/Tomahawks between them when some worn but welcome P-40K's arrived along with some experienced pilots from the Panama Canal Zone. Not that it mattered much just then. They were all grounded for 33 days without gasoline. But gradually, as the Air Transport Command got men and transports to fly the Hump (Himalayas), bringing supplies from bases in India, CATF gained strength. In March, 1943, it became part of the 14th Air Force as Chennault was promoted to major general. During its nine months of operation, CATF fighters destroyed 149 enemy planes and had 85 probables in exchange for 16 Tomahawks, P-40E's and K's.

During the summer of 1943, the 1st Chinese-American Composite Wing, consisting of the 3rd and 5th FG's, of four squadrons each, was formed and supplied mostly with P-40K's, but the 23rd FG remained the hard core of the 14th Air Force, which largely controlled

Col. Bruce K. Holloway (R) and his crew chief with their P-40 at Yunanyi, China, 23rd FG. General Holloway was boss of the Strategic Air Command in 1970. He was credited with 13 air victories in WW-II.

Photo: USAF

the air over its part of Southeast Asia by the time the 23rd began receiving some P-51 Mustangs in April, 1944. The 51st and 80th FG's continued to fly P-40's (along with some P-38's). In December, 1944, 205 Hawks were still in combat with the 14th Air Force in the China-Burma-India Theatre (CBI), and 62 of those remained as late as July, 1945.

Your authors talked with many ex-P-40 pilots while gathering material for this work, and we never found one — from "Killer" Caldwell to General Bruce Holloway — who didn't have words of praise for the one U.S. fighter that fought the entire war — especially, the tough part at the beginning against great odds. For example, General Holloway, boss of the Strategic Air Command in 1970, was a colonel in 1943, with 13 victories and C.O. of the 23rd and he had this to say: "...a lot of us are alive today because of its (P-40) ruggedness and diving speed. Almost always, we were heavily outnumbered by the Japanese and inevitably took some hits. Sometimes our P-40's came back from a combat mission so full of holes you almost had to put them against a dark background to see them — but still flying."

Curtiss-Wright assembly line, Plant No. 2, Buffalo, N.Y., 1942. P-40E's in foreground; C-46 Commandos in background.

Photo: Authors' collection

The Hawk XP-46A, Feb. 13, 1941. Smaller than the P-40, without armament or armor, it had a speed of 410 mph. Sister XP-46, with eight .30 cal guns in wings plus two fifties in nose, heavily armored, was 40 mph slower and a maintenance headache so the lightweight (5,470 lbs) design was abandoned.

Photo: Authors' collection

Above, pilots of the 26th Fighter Squadron, 51st FG, Lilibari Field, Assam, India, March 17, 1943. Kneeling: Capt. William W. Moore, Lts. Horace C. Adkins and John J. Harrington, Chaplain. Standing center: Lts. John J. Ferguson, John F. Coonan, Arthur L. Gregg, Virgil O. Burge, Alfred Wipf, William R. Rogers. On wing: Lts. Leonard C. Hicks, Larry D. Howie and Charles D. Evans. Below, Herbert O. Fisher, C-W production test pilot, went to CBI Theatre to trouble-shoot mechanical ills of C-46's and flew 50 missions with U.S. fighter units seeking ways to improve the Warhawks. He is pictured above in a P-40F. The Merlin-powered Hawks lacked air scoop atop cowl.

Photos: USAF and Port of New York Authority

Hawks also fought in the Aleutians in the worst of all possible flying weather; and helped eject, in July, 1943, enemy invaders that had occupied Attu and Kiska a year earlier. These P-40's, mostly

Poor old "War Weary," a P-40K that served her tour of duty in combat only to get pranged at Kunming, China on the way to a Chinese pilot training unit.

Photo: USAF

E models, were flown by the 11th, 18th and 54th Squadrons of the 343rd FG, a part of the 11th Air Force, from primitive bases at Adak, Amchitka, Shemya and Attu. In 1944, the 344th Squadron moved to Shemya, flying P-40M's, K's and a few D's.

Meanwhile, after the decisive U.S. Navy victory over much superior enemy forces at Midway in June, 1942, America and her allies in the Pacific were able to think about offense instead of defense for a change, and begin the long march to victory over "one damned island after another." It started in August, 1942, with the seizure of Guadalcanal and the measured advance through the Solomons by Admiral Nimitz' Central Pacific Forces, and MacArthur's concurrent 1,300-mile offensive which saw his Southwest Pacific Forces fight from Port Moresby to Hollandia on New Guinea's north coast, and beyond to the island bases of Wakde, Biak and finally Morotai, just 250 miles southeast of Mindanao. As these two great forces came together, with four large U.S. Navy task groups operating from newly-won bases in the Palaus, Yap and Ulithi, their power was merged for the invasion of the Philippines at Leyte in October, 1944. After that came the invasions of Iwo Jima and Okinawa as the last steps before the final defeat of Japan by General LeMay's B-29's with their awesome fire-bomb raids on the enemy's principal cities.

Throughout the twin campaigns in the central and southwest Pacific, the Central Pacific Forces under Admiral Nimitz had, in addition to Naval and Marine airpower, General Thomas White's 7th and General Nathan Twining's 13th Air Forces, while MacArthur ad-

69

Above, The 51st FG adopted its own fearsome mouth on its P-40K's. Lt. McClurg is preparing to deliver a 500-pounder to Japanese in Burma from 51st's base at Dinjan, India. Below, Pilots of the 89th and 90th Fighter Squadrons, 80th FG, at Dinjan, India, Aug. 15, 1944. L to R, Lts. Ralph E. Ward, Jr., Gale H. Lyon, J.B. Patton; F/O S.E. Hammer, Lts. R.D. Bell, P.A. Marshall, R.B. McReynolds and H.H. Doughty. Between them, they had a total of 19 victories at the time.

Photos: USAF

Major John Chennault, Gen. Chennault's eldest son, on Umnak Island, Aleutians, May, 1942. P-40E has Bengal tiger's head on nose of 28th Composite Group, 11th Air Force.
Photo: USAF

vanced beneath General Ennis Whitehead's 5th Air Force.

Units flying P-40's in the CBI and Pacific were: In the 5th Air Force, the 8th, 49th and 347th Fighter Groups plus the 312th Light Bomb Group (which also had A-20's). In the 7th Air Force, which grew from the ashes of the Hawaiian Air Force at Pearl Harbor, were the 15th and 318th Fighter Groups. The 13th Air Force had one P-40 Group, the 18th; and the 10th and 14th Air Forces possessed the 23rd, 51st and 80th Fighter Groups, and the 3rd and 5th Fighter Groups of the 1st Chinese-American Composite Wing, along with the 8th Photo Reconnaissance Group (82nd and 110th Reconnaissance Squadrons), all P-40 equipped. The 11th Air Force in the Aleutians contained the 343rd Fighter Group which flew P-40's, and the 28th Composite Group.

Africa and Italy

Five U.S. Hawk-equipped fighter groups, plus the 99th Fighter Squadron, fought in North Africa following Operation Torch, the Allied invasion on November 8, 1942, in which American troops went ashore near Casablanca while American and British troops simultaneously landed near Oran and Algiers.

Actually, the 57th Fighter Group had been sent to Palestine three months before and had fought alongside RAF Kittyhawk units over Libya, and then the Battle of El Alamein in October. The 57th was composed of the 64th, 65th and 66th Fighter Squadrons, and was equipped with P-40K's and F's. At this time, the 57th was part of General Lewis Brereton's 9th Air Force, operating under General Montgomery's air commander, Lord Tedder.

71

Warhawk two-place fighter trainer was made from a P-40N-30.

Photo: USAF

The 33rd FG, in support of Torch, was launched from two small catapult carriers, *HMS Archer* and the *USS Chenango,* landing at Casablanca and Port Lyautey in French Morocco. The 33rd's three squadrons, 58th, 59th and 60th, soon moved to Thelepte, Tunisia to fight with the 57th FG. These were joined by the 325th FG (the famed "Checkertail Clan"), the 79th FG (from which the 325th got its nucleus), and the 324th FG early in 1943. The Checkertail Squadrons were the 317th, 318th and 319th. The 79th FG was made up of the 85th, 86th and 87th Fighter Squadrons; and the 324th FG contained the 314th, 315th and 316th Fighter Squadrons.

The 99th Fighter Squadron — which was attached to no Fighter Group — was the first and, at the time, the only all-black squadron in the USAAF. It went into action in June, 1943, with 27 P-40L's after the Axis defeat in North Africa. Flying from bases in Tunisia, Sicily and Italy, it took part in the Pantelleria, Sicilian and Italian campaigns. At the time, the 99th's combat record was downgraded back home, but that was an injustice to a proud and gutty little (30 pilots) bunch who had obtained their wings under difficult circumstances at best. Commanded by Colonel Benjamin O. Davis,* and indoctrinated for combat by Colonel Phil Cochran, the legendary "Mr. P-40" of the 33rd's 60th Fighter Squadron ("Colonel Flip Corkin" in Milt Caniff's "Terry and the Pirates;" today, president of Lyons Transportation Company), the 99th should be judged as

72

Socrates' wife (when a friend asked the Greek philosopher how Socrates' wife was, the great thinker replied, "Compared to what?"). Compared to white fighter squadrons in the same theatre of war, the 99th's record was very good. Relatively few U.S. aces emerged from these campaigns, primarily because, after Allied victory in North Africa, the Me 109's — which were definitely inferior to the P-40's below 15,000 feet — usually refused to come down from higher altitudes — where the Me 109 was superior — and mix it up with the P-40's. In this theatre, RAF Spitfires and USAAF P-38's flew the high missions and the P-40's were ordered to remain below 15,000 as a rule, where they performed a lot of ship, bridge and truck-busting missions. In 1944, Colonel Ben Davis formed the 332nd Fighter Group of black pilots (which the 99th eventually joined), and this group, equipped with P-39's and, finally, P-51's, fought in Italy then in the China-Burma-India theatre. Total combat score for the Negro airmen was 111 confirmed victories, plus all of their bombing and strafing missions.

Following the Axis defeat in North Africa, the Italian island of Pantelleria fell to the Allies in June, 1943, and then Sicily in August. The invasion of Italy itself — just three miles across the Straits of Messina from Sicily — began September 3, 1943, and though the Italians formally surrendered five days later, German forces in Italy under Rommel and Kesserling occupied Rome and dug-in north of a defensive line that roughly divided the country in half.

The Checkertails (325th FG), gave up their P-40's to the 324th FG after the Sicilian Campaign and moved to Italy where they remained until VE Day flying P-47's and P-51's.

The 57th, 79th and 324th Fighter Groups, which were part of the 9th Air Force, by then under command of General Hoyt Vandenberg, moved to Italy in October, 1943, and soon gave up their P-40's.

The veteran 33rd FG fought in Italy until February, 1944, then went on to the China-Burma-India theatre and continued to fly P-40 Warhawks until, near the end of the Pacific War, they were equipped with P-47 Thunderbolts, a few P-38 Lightnings, and finally, P-51 Mustangs.

British Commonwealth

A number of very large and very exciting books could be (and have

*Davis was the USAF's only Negro general when he retired in 1970. Late that year, he directed the "Air Marshal" program which placed specially-trained armed men in U.S. airliners to prevent sky-jacking.

been) written about the exploits of British Commonwealth pilots who flew Tomahawks and Kittyhawks during WW-II. Space limits us in this little book to the briefest mentions of their units.

The first Tomahawks delivered to Britain were 142 H81-A1's (same as first P-40's, but with one .30 caliber gun in each wing in addition to the pair of nose guns), which had been ordered by French collapse in June, 1940. The RAF designated these machines Tomahawk Mk I's and used them mostly as fighter trainers — with RAF Squadrons 2, 13, 26, 94, 171, 239, 268 and 400 — because lack of armor, inadequate firepower and lack of performance above 15,000 feet left the Tomahawk definitely inferior to the Spitfire for the missions then demanded of British fighters.*

One hundred and ten Tomahawk Mk II and IIA's were delivered to the RAF ($35,841. each less engines, instruments and guns according to C-W billing records) during November, 1940. These

Following the invasion of North Africa, the U.S. supplied 25 Merlin-powered P-40F Warhawks to the Free French late in November, 1942. The Groupe Lafayette (II/5, formerly equipped with H75's) is pictured on Maison Blanche Airfield, Algiers, Jan. 9, 1943, en route to Tunisia.

Photo: UPI Newspictures

*British and U.S. fighter airplane philosophies never completely agreed. The RAF rejected both the early Mustang and the Lightning while openly snickering at the big 12,000-lb Thunderbolt. The nimble Spitfire was unquestionably one of the best fighters of WW-II, but it lacked the ruggedness that brought many a pilot home from battle in a shot-up Hawk or Thunderbolt.

Above, Tomahawk Mk IIA of RAAF Squadron No. 3 which fought the Desert War. Armorers are re-loading guns as Aussie pilot inspects landing gear. Below, Australian Ace (17 victories) Squadron Leader K.W. "Bluey" Truscott in his Kittyhawk IA at Gurney Field, Milne Bay, Papua, in August, 1942. Truscott led RAAF No. 76 Squadron.

Photos: RAAF via Barry Pattison and RAAF

were H81-A2's, similar to the P-40B, with two .303 Browings in each
wing, plus the pair of "fifties" in the nose. Twenty-four of these
craft were given to Russia and the remainder served with the Mk
I's as trainers and as reconnaissance machines.

Also during November, 1940, the RAF began receiving the
Tomahawk Mk IIB, the Curtiss Model H81-A3, similar to the P-40C.
Externally, the P-40C and Tomahawk Mk IIB was identical to the
P-40B; but internally, incorporated a new fuel system with larger,
improved self-seling tanks and fittings for an external (belly) auxil-
lary tank of 52 gallons. Both the P-40C and the Tomahawk Mk IIB
had four wing guns, though MK IIB serials AN517 and 50 machines
from the AM370-AM519 range had six wing-mounted .303's and no
nose guns (the remaining 100 airplanes of this 150-plane serial range
were H81-A2's sent to the AVG and were never actually delivered
to Britain).

In Britain, Mk IIB's served with RAF Squadrons 2, 26, 73, 136,
168, 239,241, 403, 414, 430 and 616. This model Tomahawk served
in the Desert War with RAF Squadrons 112, 250 and 274. Also in
the Middle East were South African Air Force (RAAF) Squadron 3,

**RAAF maintenance depot tending white-tailed Kittyhawks of #76 Squadron (SV) and #80
Squadron (BU). SV-H is a Kittyhawk III, Lend-Lease P-40M-10, s/n A29-357.**

Photo: RAAF via Barry Pattison

Kittyhawk IV's of No. 84 Squadron, RAAF, over Horn Island, 1944. In foreground is a P-40N-20 with squared-off rear canopy and cut-down aft deck; others are earlier N Models.
Photo: Merle C. Olmsted Collection

all equipped with Tomahawk IIB's.

About 300 Tomahawks were sent to these squadrons fighting Rommel in the Western Desert, but most were shipped to Takoradi on Africa's Gold Coast, assembled there and flown across the Sahara to Cairo then to desert airstrips, and at least forty were lost in transit.

The Commonwealth Tomahawks fought in North Africa — the "Desert War" — throughout 1941, with RAF 112 Squadron, led by a big, deadly Australian, Clive "Killer" Caldwell. Then, in the late fall of 1941, the new Kittyhawks began to arrive to replace the Tomahawks.

The Kittyhawk was the Curtiss-Wright Model Hawk 87 (H87), and it was fitted with the Allison V-1710-39 engine with an external spur prop reduction gear which shortened the nose and raised the propeller thrust line. Fuselage cross-section was reduced and the canopy re-designed. At a glance, the easiest way to different-iate between the Kittyhawk and Tomahawk was to compare noses: The Kittyhawk had a much deeper radiator scoop which was moved forward, and the upper nose decking curved very little to the higher-positioned prop. Landing gear legs were also shortened. The

An obviously well-experienced Warhawk is this P-40N-20, s/n 43-24118, Lt. Walt Witbeck flying from a training base in Florida, 1944.

Photo: Francis H. Dean Collection

first Kittyhawk was the same as the P-40D (for more details, see PART 6).

The Royal New Zealand Air Force (RNZAF), with only one combat squadron in December, 1941, was equipped with Kittyhawks (Models E, M, N and apparently, a single L); and at its peak had a total of 13 fighter squadrons, seven of these flying Kittyhawks. The RNZAF acquired 293 Kittyhawks; using squadrons were 14, 15, 16, 17, 18, 19 and 20. New Zealand's pilots fought mainly in the New Guinea Campaign, over Bougainville and across the South Pacific under their own flag; but, like the Aussies, actually fought everywhere in RAF squadrons.

Until the end of 1942, much of the burden of defense in the Southwest Pacific fell upon the Australians. It was not enough that the Aussies supplied many of the men and much of the guts for the Desert War half a-world away, but in late December, the Japanese had blasted right up to Australia's back door — while the Allied grand strategy of "Beat Hitler First" kept the Aussies hamstrung and many of their best fighting men scattered in all major war theatres serving with other Commonwealth units. Only in the Southwest Pacific area did Australian flyers fight under their own senior officers, and even there — in the interest of unified command — their senior officers were under an American air commander, General George Kenney, who in turn answered to General MacArthur.

But no matter who did the bossing the Aussies were merely fantastic fighters whatever the theatre and whatever the conditions. Curtiss-Wright test pilot, Gerrardus "Jerry" Clark, who checked-out Australian and New Zealand pilots in Hawks, put it this way: "Those wild Aussies, and later the New Zealanders, were the roughest guys I ever saw. They were wonderful fighting men and they flew those Hawks day-in, day-out, no matter what. They never showed fear, and if that P-40 would go, even at half-power, those men would fly it right into the teeth of any combat."

At the peak, the RAAF had 13 fighter squadrons of its own. Eight of these were equipped with Kittyhawks. Starting with #75, #76 and #77 Squadrons in mid-March, 1942, RAAF Kittyhawks clashed repeatedly with the Japanese from Port Moresby and Milne Bay. Later, sharing the entire Southwest Pacific area (New Guinea. Philippines, Borneo, Java, Tasmania and the Northern Solomons) with the USAAF's 5th Air Force, RAAF Kittyhawk Squadrons #78, #80, #82, #84 and #86 were added in 1943-44. Joined by the Dutch Kittyhawk Squadron, Netherlands East Indies #120 which had trained in Australia, they strafed and escorted, bombed, skip-bombed and hunted the enemy. They returned to the Philippines with MacArthur and, as late as July 23, 1945, the Aussies Kitty bombed a final target in Borneo. Kittyhawks remained on strength with RAAF Squadrons #75, #78 and #80 until the peace treaty with Japan was signed.

A total of 2,091 P-40's of several models went to the Soviets during WW-II. Those squadron records, if any Free World researcher ever gets to them, will undoubtedly add many more proud chapters to the story of the Hawks.

The debate will of course continue among aviation historians attempting to establish just which fighter airplane was "best" during WW-II. It matters little, except for a given time or condition. But certain things cannot be denied: the Hawks were rugged and they were there — and a lot of Allied fighting men are here because of that.

P-40 AIRFRAMES

The P-40 series airframe was basically the same as the P-36. Fuselage was monocoque, built in two halves and joined at center-line. Internal structure was bulkhead and stringer, skin was 24S1 aluminum alloy. The wing was in four sections. The main panels bolted to the fuselage but carried through the fuselage and were mated at the center with bridge-type splice-plates which made for unusual strength. Wingtips were removable. Ailerons, rudder and elevators were fabric-covered. Tail-wheel was fully retractable and covered by doors. The eleven-foot propeller was electrically controlled constant-speed. The automatic engine-cooling system utilized a pair of radiators, placed with the oil cooler beneath the nose in the large scoop which was fitted with cowl flaps. Main fuel tank (61.25 gal) and reserve (40.5) were in wings. Fuselage tank, aft of pilot, had 57 gal capacity.

The XP-40 was powered with the Allison V-1710-19. P-40 through P-40C airframe was billed at $22,929 ea for first 200; then $33,429.71 for next 325 units. Engines began at about $15,000 each, but dropped to $9,000 each in mid-war. Props, instruments armament, and radios added approximately $3,000 more per craft.

Beginning with the H87 series, P-40D and onward, nose guns were removed and six "fifties" in the wings became more or less standard armament (though some pilots preferred four guns with additional ammunition). Actually, the D Model was designed for four fifties and provision for two 20-mm cannon; but most became Kittyhawks and received four guns at the factory, with two more sometimes added in the field.

The E Model provided for two 100-lb wing bombs, plus a 500-pounder under belly; had 175 lbs more armor and beefed-up internal wing structure to carry heavier external stores.

The P-40F and onward were called "Warhawks;" possessed 170 gal belly tank; Merlin engine. Merlin-powered Hawks were quickly recognizable by lack of air scoop atop cowl. P-40F-5 had lenghtened fuselage (to 33′ 4″) and rudder and fin moved rearward of horizontal tail. P-40F-10 had manually-operated cowl flaps. P-40F-15 had winterization items. P-40F-20 added demand-type oxygen system. Airframe price up to $38,296 for F Models.

P-40K-1 was similar to E, with short fuselage; large fillet around vertical fin and V-1710-73 engine. P-40K-5 same as K-1 except for addition of rotary valve cooler. P-40K-10 same as earlier K's except for lengthened fuselage; some winterized. P-40K-15 long fuselage, winterized; emergency hydraulic system eliminated; battery moved forward.

P-40L-1, planned as lightweight F's with Merlin engine; two guns per wing; short fuselage. P-40L-5, same as L-1 with long fuselage; two guns per wing plus rocket fittings. P-40L-10, long fuselage; aux fuel pump relocated; armor removed from coolant tank; several warning lights removed from panel, and sway braces added for 75 gal belly tank. P-40L-15, same as L-10 but with permanent carb air filter and provision for interior signal light. P-40L-20, new radio (SCR-695), improved relays and provision for installation of incendiary grenade.

P-40M-1, developed from the K, Allison V-1710-81; cooling grill added forward of exhaust stubs; long fuselage. P-40M-5, same as M-1 with re-inforced ailerons and permanent carb air filter. P-40M-10, same as M-5 but with fuel pressure warning signal, air vapor eliminator and visual landing gear indicator (colored pin on upper surface of each wing) replacing gear warning horn.

P-40N-1, airframe price up to $44,892. Fastest Warhawk at 378 mph; headrest armor restored; small wing tanks removed; lighter wheels and aluminum radiator and oil cooler. V-1710-81 engine with automatic boost control. P-40N-5, same as N-1, but new SCR-696 radio, new pilot's seat and external stores fittings restored. P-40N-10, same as N-5 but with winterization items; two guns per wing. P-40N-15, three guns per wing and 137 gal wing tanks restored. P-40N-20, Modified canopy and deeper fuselage cut-out with squared-off aft canopy for improved vision to rear; six wing guns and provision for three 500-lb bombs. P-40N-25, fitted with V-1710-99 Allison; new non-metal self-sealing tanks. P-40N-30, V-1710-99 Allison; minor equipment changes; two converted to two-place trainers and re-designated TP-40N-30's. P-40N-35, V-1710-99 engine; new radio and ADF; minor instrument changes. P-40N-40, V-1710-115 Allison; this final order was for 1,000 machines, but last 784 cancelled. Re-located armor; new oxygen system; flame-suppressing exhaust stacks; automatic boost and prop control.

The XP-40Q was taken out of the production P-40N-25's (s/n 43-24571) and was given a bubble canopy with cut-down rear deck; wing radiators and four-bladed prop. Further experimentation included the XP-40Q-1, XP-40Q-2 and XP-40Q-3, modified K's, with clipped wings and various engine installations. None were developed.

NOTE: Specifications for P-40 engines and for the following models: P-40, P-40B, P-40C, P-40D, P-40E & E-1, P-40F, P-40L, P-40K, P-40M, and P-40N appear on pages 82 and 83.

P-40 ENGINES

The Rolls Royce Merlin Model 28, V-1650-1, was built in the U.S. by Packard during WW-II. Bore and stroke was 5x6" giving a displacement of 1,649 cu. in. Its single-stage, two-speed geared supercharger had ratios of 8.151:1, and 9.490:1. Compression ratio was 6:1, and this engine weighed 1,520 lbs dry.

	Horsepower	RPMS	Altitude
Take-off	1,300	3,000	sea level
Military	1,240	3,000	11,500 ft
	1,120	3,000	18,500
Continuous	1,000	2,650	sea level
	1,080	2,650	9,500
	1,010	2,650	16,000

The Allison V-1710, built by the Allison Division of GM, had a bore and stroke of 5.5x6" giving a displacement of 1,710 cu. in. Compression ratio was 6.65:1. These engines ranged in weight from 1,310 lbs (V-1710-33) to 1,385 lbs (V-1710-115).

Power Settings	Engine Model	Horse-power	RPM	Altitude
Take-off	V-1710-33	1,040*	3,000	sea level
	V-1710-39	1,150*	3,000	sea level
	V-1710-73	1,325*	3,000	sea level
	-81, -99, -115	1,200*	3,000	sea level
War Emergency	V-1710-39	1,470*	3,000	sea level
	V-1710-73	1,550*	3,000	sea level
	-81, -99, -115	1,360*	3,000	sea level
Maximum Cruise 75%	V-1710-33	715	2,300	10,000 ft
	V-1710-39 & -73	750	2,300	10,800
	V-1710-81	750	2,300	14,000
	V-1710-99 & -115	750	2,300	16,500

*For five minutes only   All mixture settings auto-rich

USAAF	P-40	P-40B	P-40C	P-40D	P-40E & E-1
Curtiss-Wright	H81-A	H81-A2	H81-A2	H87-A2	H87-A3
	H81-A1		H81-A3		H87-A4
Commonwealth	Tomahawk Mk I*	Mk II	Mk IIB	Kittyhawk Mk I	Mk IA
Wing span	37′ 4″	37′ 4″	37′ 4″	37′ 4″	37′ 4″
Wing area	236 sq. ft.	236	236	236	236
Length	31′ 8½″	31′ 8½″	31′ 8½″	31′ 2″	31′ 2″
Gross weight	7,215 lbs	7,645	8,058	8,809	9,200
Empty weight	5,376	5,590	5,812	6,208	6,350
Fuel capacity	180 internal	160	160	148	157
Maximum speed	357 mph	352	345	350	354
Initial climb	3,080 fpm	2,860	2,650	2,580	2,050
Landing speed	80 mph	80	85	85	85
Service ceiling	32,750 ft	32,400	29,500	30,600	29,000
Range	950 mi	730	730	650	700
Engine	V-1710-33	V-1710-33	V-1710-33	V-1710-39	V-1710-39

* Tomahawk Mk IA and IB basically the same as Tomahawk Mk I with changes in instruments and radios.

USAAF	P-40F	P-40L	P-40K	P-40M	P-40N
Curtiss-Wright	H87-B3	H87-B4	H87*	H87*	H87-V & W
Commonwealth	Kittyhawk Mk II	Mk II	Mk III	Mk III	Mk IV
Wing span	37′ 4″	37′ 4″	37′ 4″	37′ 4″	37′ 4″
Wing area	236 sq ft	236	236	236	236
Length	31′ 8½″†	31′ 8½″‡	31′ 8½″§	33′ 4″	33′ 4″
Gross weight	9,350 lbs**	9,000	10,000	8,900	8,850
Empty weight	6,590 lbs	6,340	6,400	5,454	6,000
Fuel capacity	149 gal	149	157	157	158
Maximum speed	364 mph	364	362	360	378*†
Initial climb	2,200 fpm	2,400	2,000	2,050	2,120
Landing speed	82 mph	80	82	82	82
Service ceiling	34,400 ft	34,400	28,000	30,000	31,000
Range	815 mi	815	700	700	750
Engine	V-1650-1	V-1650-1	V-1710-73	V-1710-81	V-1710-81
					V-1710-99
					V-1710-115

*C-W Billing lists no dash number
†P-40F-10 thru F-20, 33′ 4″
‡P-40L-5 thru L-20, 33′ 4″

§P-40K-10 thru K-15, 33′ 4″
**With belly tank, 9,870 lbs
*†P-40N-5 thru P-40N-40, 350 mph

Thirty P-40N's were modified for photo-reconnaissance; two modified to two-place trainers.

P-1D Hawk of the 43rd School Squadron, Kelly Field. The bumbled bee insignia, outlined in yellow, carries the legend, "Cielito Lindo, Mexico," and the aircraft weights, fuel and oil capacities and rigging data are stenciled beneath cockpit. Wings were chrome yellow; struts and fuselage and fin olive drab; horizontal tail surfaces chrome yellow.

Photo courtesy Merle C. Olmsted Collection

Army Biplanes, Color: The Hawk P-1 through P-1C were solid camouflage brown (dark khaki) overall. After passage of the Air Corps Act in July, 1926, beginning with the P-1D (AT-4), Hawks began coming from the factory with chrome-yellow wings and horizontal tail; and olive drab fuselage, fin and struts. In 1935, the Hawks still in service — mostly P-6E's — had the olive drab on fuselage, fin and struts replaced with light blue, while the chrome-yellow surfaces became orange-yellow at that time.

Army Biplanes, Markings: Hawks P-1 through P-1C bore the star-in-circle national insignias on top and bottom wings full-chord in size and as near the tips as possible. Beginning with the P-1D, these insignias were reduced in size on the upper wings and positioned between leading edge and ailerons. The P-1 through P-1C rudder bore three vertical stripes of equal width, with blue adjacent to the rudder post, white in center and red next to the rudder trailing edge. Beginning with the P-1D, the rudder carried a wide blue vertical stripe next to the rudder post with 13 alternating red and white horizontal bars extending to the rudder's trailing edge. Also, beginning with the P-1D, the under surfaces of the lower wings carried the legend "U.S." (starboard) "ARMY" (port) inboard of the star insignias.

Army Biplanes, Serials & Numbers: Air Service P-1's through P-1C's had the aircraft serial positioned on each side of the fuselage near the tail in four or six-inch block letters, while the make and model of the aircraft appeared on each side of the rudder near the top. After July, 1926, make and model data were moved to the aft fuselage with the serial, and "U.S. Army" added to make a three-line descriptive block. In 1931, this information was reduced in size to one-inch characters and positioned (usually) just ahead of the cockpit on the left side of the fuselage.

Individual aircraft numbers within each Air Corps Group were painted on the vertical fin or (in larger size) on each side of the fuselage behind the cockpit during the late twenties and thirties, except for the Hawks of the 43rd School Squadron at Kelly Field which displayed these numbers on each side of the engine cowlings. Originally, these numbers ran from "1" upward within each Group, although early in 1929 the Hawks of the First Pursuit Group began to take the airplane number from the last two digits (or last three digits if the same number should be repeated) of the aircraft serial number.

Also, during the late twenties, many Hawks carried a nine-inch shield painted on each side of the tunnel radiator which contained the names of pilot and crew chief.

Army P-36's, Color: In 1928, the Air Corps accepted Ford Trimotors in natural aluminum finish; but the Y1P-36's (and Seversky P-35's) purchased in 1936 were its first fighters to enter service in natural aluminum. This practice was followed with subsequent tactical aircraft until early in 1940 when P-40's coming off the assembly lines were painted overall a brownish olive drab with medium gray undersides. Beginning in March, 1941, the P-36's in service received this same camouflage paint scheme.

Army P-36's, Markings: Squadron insignias disappeared from P-36's when camouflage paint was applied beginning in March, 1941, and the rudder stripes were eliminated at this time. The star-in-circle national insignia was applied to all four wing surfaces near the tips, and to each side of the fuselage. In June, 1942, the red center was removed from the star insignia and this insignia was carried only on the lower right and upper left wings. In July, 1943, white rectangular bars were added to the white star-in-blue-circle (today's insignia, which has a red stripe in the center of each of the rectangular bars, was adopted in January, 1947 — by which time no Hawks remained in service).

When the P-36A's entered service in 1938, a "designator," consisting of two letters above two numbers, each two-character block eight inches high, was applied to both sides of the fin, on the left-upper wing and on under surface of left wing between the leading edge and the word "Army." The letters were PA, PH, PP, PR and PT, representing each Pursuit Group by matching the second letter with its numerical sequence in the alphabet to the Group number. For example, since T is the 20th letter of the alphabet, the 20th Pursuit Group was "PT." The two numbers of this designator system identified individual airplanes within each Group, with 0 to 10 assigned to headquarters, 11 to 39 for the first squadron, 40 to 69 the middle squadron and 70 to 99 the third squadron. These numbers were usually repeated on both sides of the engine cowling. But this was clearly a clumsy way of doing things and this system was abandoned in January, 1940, when the US Air Corps began adding many more groups.

That new system, which retained the designators in the same positions on the aircraft and in the same size characters, placed the airplane number at the top of the combination; and the Group designation simply became the actual Group number. For example, the 20th Pursuit Group was shown as "20P."

Army Air Corps/Air Forces P-40's, Color: All USAAC/USAAF P-40's were delivered in one of three paint schemes. Most were olive drab overall with light gray undersides (some were dappled in medium green); the others were delivered in desert pink overall; and some — particularly those of the 14th Air Force — were randomly camouflaged in dark brown and desert pink.

In 1943, the 45th Squadron of the 15th Fighter Group (7th Air Force, Pacific) painted its P-40's light gray overall. The 49th Squadron of the 80th Fighter Group in the Far East Air Force (1944) originally possessed black-and-white checkered tails and white prop spinners, later changed to solid white tails with a narrow red band around the rear fuselage separating the white and olive drab. In addition, these craft wore a white stripe on the underside of each wing running from the root's leading edge to the trailing edge near the tip, plus a fuselage stripe just behind the cockpit.

The 325th Fighter Group in North Africa had the tail surfaces of its P-40's painted a checkerboard of black and yellow, with the pattern applied diagonally, and its prop spinners red, yellow or white according to squadron.

The 332nd Fighter Group in Italy included the 99th Fighter Squadron, the all-Negro Squadron that had previously fought its P-40's from Sicily, and this Group adopted solid red tails.

Army Air Corps/Air Forces P-40's, Markings: The first P-40's were delivered during the late summer of 1940 and carried the old star-in-circle-with-red-center national insignia on all four wing surfaces; had rudders containing the blue vertical stripe with 13 red/white bars, and the legend, "U.S. ARMY" on underwing surfaces. In March, 1941, the rudder markings disappeared and a star-in-circle was added to each side of the fuselage. In June, 1942, the red center was removed from the star and it was carried only on the lower right wing and upper left wing, though remaining on each side of the fuselage. At this time, the "U.S. ARMY" began to disappear from beneath the wing, though it was still seen late into 1943 (51st FG in India). In July, 1943, white rectangular bars were added to the star insignia. Blue borders around the rectangles were added in September, 1943.

In the late summer of 1942, P-40's in the Middle East began wearing an RAF-type fin flash consisting of three vertical bars, red/white/blue (front to back), with the white bar much narrower than the other two; and had RAF-type yellow outlines around the star insignias.

Group insignias included the tiger shark mouth and "evil eye" of the 23rd Fighter Group, which grew from the AVG (Flying Tigers). The AVG apparently borrowed this from the RAF #112 Squadron in the Mid-East, which had in turn got the idea from Luftwaffe ZG-76, an Me 110 unit that 112 Squadron had met earlier over Greece.

The 51st Group (10th Air Force) also had a shark-type mouth on its P-40's, but with one upper fang extended and curved to resemble a saber-tooth tiger.

The 80th Fighter Group chose a side view of a huge skull for each side of the cowling of its P-40's; while in the Aleutians the 11th Fighter Squadron had a stylized Bengal tiger's head on each side of the P-40's air scoop, and the 18th decorated the cowl sides with a snow eagle in flight.

Air Corps and USAAF P-40 aircraft numbers were applied according to the same system as outlined for the P-36 for comparable periods. After March, 1941, serial numbers, with the first digit of the fiscal year removed, were usually painted in white on each side of the vertical tail, sometimes on fin only, sometimes across rudder and fin.

AVG (Flying Tigers) Tomahawks, Colors & Markings: The H81-A2 Tomahawks diverted from the RAF to the Flying tigers were painted in the RAF's standard temperate land camouflage of green and brown with sky-blue undersides. Chinese National insignia was the 12-point star (white) in blue circle and was carried on all four wing surfaces. The famed shark's mouth was on all airscoops, though was noticably smaller than later such renderings because the Tomahawk had a smaller air scoop. A winged tiger was painted on both sides of some AVG craft. The tiger was yellow with black stripes, his wings pale blue.

The 1st Squadron, the "Adam and Eve," had a narrow, white fuselage stripe barely in front of the tail fin. Its squadron insignia was a couple of pale green apples encircled by a black snake upon which was lettered, in white, "The First Pursuit." White stick figures of "Eve" pursuing "Adam" decorated the apples.

The 2nd Squadron had a blue fuselage stripe just ahead of the fin and used a small, white panda bear, outlined in black, as its squadron insignia.

The 3rd Squadron, "Hell Angels," carried a red fuselage stripe, three-colored wheel covers and a variety of nude "ladies" with wings and halos.

Two-digit identification numbers, free-hand painted, were carried on each side of aft fuselage of all the original 100 Tomahawks, and a five-digit AVG number, running from P-8100 through P-8200, was positioned on the fin in small characters. Replacement P-40E's used 3-digit aircraft numbers on each side of the fuselage.

British Commonwealth Tomahawks & Kittyhawks, Colors & Markings: Prior to August, 1941, all RAF Tomahawks were painted in the temperate land camouflage of brown and green, with sky-blue undersides. At that time, the new Desert camouflage of dark-earth and mid-stone, with pale blue undersurfaces, appeared and eventually covered most Tomahawks and Kittyhawks, though some later entered service in the same shade of "Desert Pink" as USAAF P-40's in the Mid-East.

The RAAF's first Kittyhawks were standard RAF green and brown camouflage, while the RNZAF Kittyhawks were painted in the USAAF olive drab.

The RAF Tomahawks and Kittyhawks all retained the RAF fin flash of red/white/blue throughout 1940 and 1941 whether flown by the RAF, RAAF or SAAF squadrons. The RAF national insignia was a roundel of blue, white and red (outer to inner), the colors evenly proportioned until 1942. Roundels were carried on all four wing surfaces and on each side of the fuselage and were outlined in yellow. In 1942 the white middle ring was reduced greatly and the outer blue and red center propotionately enlarged. Sometimes, the yellow outline was omitted on the wing roundels. Designator letters, equal in size to the roundel, were fore and aft of the fuselage roundel on Commonwealth fighters.

Prior to 1942, RAAF roundels were equal-sized blue (outside) and white rings with a small red center, and fin flashes were white-blue-white. From 1942, RAAF roundels eliminated the red center and most of the RAAF Kittyhawks were painted with white tails.

The RNZAF roundels were light blue, white, light blue (outer to inner) outlined in yellow, with fin flashes of the same combination — though some used a pencil-thin red stripe in place of the second light blue bar. In 1943, the RNZAF began adding a white rectangular bar to each side of its roundels resulting in a national insignia similar to that adopted by the USAAF.

Commonwealth Tomahawk and Kittyhawk serials were carried, usually in eight-inch letters/numbers, on each side of the aft fuselage with two or three characters extending beneath the horizontal stabilizer.

Special markings on Commonwealth Hawks varied greatly. Some SAAF Tomahawks in North Africa had shark mouths and yellow leading edge stripes. Some spinners were painted according to squadron, while maps of Africa appeared on the cowls of some SAAF craft.

The ten Polish pilots fighting with RAF #112 Squadron painted Poland's national emblem on the tails of their Kittyhawks.

Navy & Marine Biplanes, Color: The first Navy airplanes were, like those of the Army, finished in clear dope and sometimes varnished. In 1918, most Navy service aircraft were painted standard battleship gray with wings and tail surfaces silver. Some tactical craft, particularly flying boats, received camouflage paint schemes similar to that of Navy warships. In 1920, Navy airplanes (except the solid yellow trainers) were painted silver overall with chrome yellow on the upper surfaces of the top wings and upper surfaces of the horizontal stabilizers. In the late twenties, metal parts went to light gray, then again reverted to silver in 1934. This color scheme remained standard until March, 1941, by which time the Navy and Marines no longer operated Hawks.

Navy & Marine Biplanes, Markings: At the time the Navy acquired its first Hawks, almost all Navy planes carried three vertical red-white-blue rudder stripes. But in 1926 some squadrons began painting the entire tail a solid color adopted to identify those squadrons by their own color-code. By 1928, the vertical tail stripes had disappeared on Navy fighters, although the Marines kept these stripes until March, 1941. In 1937, the solid-color tails were assigned to identify squadron service on a particular carrier. Thus, green belonged to the USS Ranger; white, USS Saratoga; yellow, USS Lexington; blue, USS Enterprise; black, USS Yorktown. The Langley's color was red, but she became a seaplane tender that year.

National insignia was painted on wings as on Army Hawks. Navy squadron numbers on each side of the fuselage combined with a separate color-code — cowl and fuselage band — in the early thirties to identify squadron, mission and plane number (for example, 5 - B - 1), while the color of the cowl and fuselage band identified each three-plane section: a solidly-painted cowl was the lead aircraft; top half of cowl in corresponding color the #2 plane; bottom half of cowl in same color, #3 plane of that section. Section colors were red, white, blue, green and yellow within each squadron — and of course, did not match the color of the tails that identified the squadron's carrier. Only the lead plane of each section carried the fuselage band.

This P-40K was photographed at Conners Park Airdrome, Rockhampton, Australia, November 4, 1942; apparently an operational casualty since no battle damage is evident.

Photo courtesy USAF

PART 6: HAWK SERIALS, DELIVERY DATES & TOTAL PRODUCED

Army Hawk Biplanes

XP-1	1 delivered	7/25; s/n 25-410
P-1	9 delivered	beginning 10/25; s/n 25-411 through 25-419
XP-2	1 delivered	1/26; s/n 25-420
P-2	4 delivered	1/26; s/n 25-421 through 25-424
P-1A	25 delivered	beginning 4/26; s/n 26-276 through 26-300
XAT-4		Conversion of P-1A s/n 26-296
XP-3		Conversion of P-1A s/n 26-300
XP-3A (#1)		Re-conversion of P-1A s/n 26-300
XP-3A (#2)		Conversion of P-3A s/n 28-189
P-1B	25 delivered	beginning 11/26; s/n 27-063 through 27-087
XP-1B		Conversion of P-1B s/n 27-071
AT-4	35 delivered	beginning 5/27; s/n 27-088 through 27-097 and 27-213 through 27-237
P-1D		Conversion of all AT-4's above
AT-5	5 delivered	beginning 7/27; s/n 27-238 through 27-242

P-1E		Conversion of four AT-5's above
XP-6		Conversion of P-2 s/n 25-423
XP-6A (#1)		Conversion of P-1A s/n 26-295
XP-6A (#2)		Conversion of P-6A s/n 29-263
P-5	5 delivered	beginning 1/28; s/n 27-327 through 27-331
XP-5		Prototype P-5 s/n 27-327 listed above
AT-5A	31 delivered	beginning 6/28; s/n 28-042 through 28-072
P-1F		Conversion of 24 of above AT-5A's
XP-10	1 delivered	8/28; s/n 28-387
XP-17		Conversion of XP-1 s/n 25-410
P-3A	5 delivered	beginning 10/28; s/n 28-189 through 28-193
P-1C	33 delivered	beginning 1/29; s/n 29-227 through 29-259
XP-1C		Conversion of P-1C s/n 29-238
XP-6B		Conversion of P-1C s/n 29-259
XP-6F	1 delivered	3/29; s/n 29-374
YP-20		Original designation of XP-6F above
P-6 or YP-6	18 delivered	beginning 10/29; s/n 29-260 through 29-273 and 29-363 through 29-366
P-6A		Conversion of seven P-6's above
P-6D		Conversion of ten P-6's above, plus two P-11's below
P-11	2 delivered	11/30; s/n 29-367 and 29-368. Converted before delivery to P-6D's
XP-22		Conversion of P-6A s/n 29-262
P-6E	45 delivered	beginning 12/31; s/n 32-233 through 32-277 (originally ordered as Y1P-22)

P-6G		Conversion of P-6E s/n 32-254
XP-6H		Conversion of P-6E s/n 32-233
XP/YP-23	1 delivered	4/32; s/n 32-278

247 TOTAL ARMY HAWK BIPLANES

Navy & Marine Hawk Biplanes

F6C-1	5 delivered	beginning 9/25; s/n A-6968 through A-6972
F6C-2	4 delivered	11/25; s/n A-6973 through A-6976
F6C-3	35 delivered	beginning 1/27; s/n A-7128 through A-7162
XF6C-3		Conversion of F6C-3 s/n A-7136
F6C-4	31 delivered	beginning 2/27; s/n A-7393 through A-7423
XF7C-1	1 delivered	8/27; s/n A-7653
F7C-1	17 delivered	beginning 8/27; s/n A-7654 through A-7670
XF6C-5		Conversion of F6C-1 s/n A-6968
F6C-6		Conversion of F6C-3 s/n A-7144
XF6C-6		Conversion of F6C-3 s/n A-7147
XF9C-1	1 delivered	3/31; s/n 8731 (Navy's "A" prefix dropped from serials in 1932)
XF11C-2 & XBFC-2	1 delivered	4/32; s/n 9213. Became the XBFC-2 in March, 1934 when designations changed.
F9C-2	6 delivered	beginning 6/32; s/n 9056 through 9061
XF11C-1 & XBFC-1	1 delivered	9/32; s/n 9219. Became the XBFC-1 in March, 1934 when designations changed
XF6C-7		Conversion of F6C-4 s/n A-7403
XF9C-2	1 delivered	1/10/33; s/n 9264

F11C-2 & BFC-2	27 delivered	beginning 3/33; s/n 9266 through 9282 and 9331 through 9340. Became BFC-2 3/34.
XF11C-3 & XBF2C-1		Conversion of F11C-2 s/n 9269. Became XBF2C-1 in March, 1934 when Navy designations changed.
BF2C-1	27 delivered	beginning 10/34; s/n 9586 through 9611 plus one unknown serial, probably 9612

157 TOTAL NAVY & MARINE BIPLANE HAWKS

Export Biplane Hawks

ARGENTINA

Hawk III	10 delivered	beginning 5/36; s/n 12085 through 12094
Hawk IV	1 delivered	7/36; s/n unknown

BOLIVIA

P-1	4 delivered	purchased in 1927. No other info
Hawk II	6 delivered	beginning 12/32; s/n H-23 through H-26 plus H-64 and H-65
Hawk II Sea	3 delivered	6/34; s/n SH-27 through SH-29

CHILE

P-1A	8 delivered	in 1926; serials unknown
P-1B	8 delivered	in 1927; serials unknown
Hawk II Sea	3 delivered	1/35; s/n SH-7 through SH-9
Hawk II	1 delivered	3/35; s/n 11767

CHINA

Hawk II	50 delivered	beginning 3/33; s/n H-47 through H-63, H-66 through H-79; first 19 serials unknown
Hawk III	102 delivered	beginning 3/36; s/n 12095 through 12155; 12175 through 12185; 12726 through 12755

COLOMBIA

Hawk II Sea	26 delivered	beginning 10/32; s/n SH-3 through SH-6; SH-10 through SH-25; SH-30 through SH-35

CUBA

P-6S	3 delivered	in 1930; serials unknown
Hawk II	4 delivered	1/33; s/n H-19 through H-22

GERMANY

Hawk II	2 delivered	10/33; s/n H-80 and H-81

JAPAN

P-1A	1 delivered	in 1927; serial unknown
P-6S	1 delivered	in 1930; serial unknown

NETHERLANDS EAST INDIES

P-6	8 delivered	9/30; serials unknown. Retroactively called Hawk I

NORWAY

Hawk II	1 delivered	7/34; serial unknown

SIAM (THAILAND)

Hawk II	12 delivered	beginning 8/34; s/n H-85 through H-96
Hawk III	24 delivered	beginning 8/35; s/n 12061 through 12083

TURKEY

Hawk II	19 delivered	beginning 8/32; serials unknown
Hawk III	1 delivered	4/35; s/n 11924

OTHERS

Hawk III	1 delivered	9/34; s/n 11894. Probably a demonstrator, listed only to "C-W Export."
P-6S	1 delivered;	civil registration NR982V, Al Williams Gulfhawk; modified and later called Hawk 1A

P-6	1 delivered;	civil registration NX9110, Jess Bristow's Essohawk, originally a C-W company demonstrator flown by Jimmy Doolittle

301 TOTAL EXPORT HAWK BIPLANES (includes two U.S. civilian Hawks)

U.S. Army Air Corps/Air Forces Hawks, Model 75, P-36, P-37 & P-42

Y1P-36	3 delivered	3 and 4/37; s/n 37-068 through 37-070
XP-37	1 delivered	4/37; s/n 37-375
P-36A	176 delivered	beginning 4/38; s/n 38-001 through 38-003; 38-005 through 38-009; 38-011 through 38-019; 38-021 through 38-084 and 38-086 through 38-180
P-36B	1 delivered	11/38; s/n 38-020
H75R	1 delivered	1/39; C-W s/n 12931; company demo, civil registration NX22028
XP-42	1 delivered	4/39; s/n 38-004
P-36C	31 delivered	4/39; s/n 38-085 and 38-181 through 38-210
XP-36D		Conversion of P-36A s/n 38-174
XP-36E		Conversion of P-36A s/n 38-147
XP-36F		Conversion of P-36A s/n 38-172
YP-37	13 delivered	beginning 4/39; s/n 38-472 through 38-484
P36G	30 delivered	beginning 5/42; s/n 42-38305 through 42-38322 and 42-108995 through 42-109006. These were H75A-8's ordered by Norway taken over by USAAF

241 TOTAL P-36's to AIR CORPS/USAAF
 1 AIR CORPS DEMONSTRATOR NX22028 (H75R)
 1 MODEL 75 PROTOTYPE NX17Y (not listed above)
 14 TOTAL P-37's to AIR CORPS
 1 XP-42 to AIR CORPS

Export Hawk 75's and Mohawks

ARGENTINA

H75-H	1 delivered	6/37; s/n (C-W) 12328
H75-0	29 delivered	11 and 12/38; s/n 12769 through 12797
H75-0	20 delivered	1940; built in Argentina under license

CHINA

H75-H	1 delivered	6/37; s/n (C-W) 12327
H75-M	30 delivered	beginning 5/38; s/n (C-W) 12625 through 12654
H75-Q	1 delivered	11/38; s/n (C-W) 12898; retract gear

Note: Although a C-W public relations release, dated 1946, claimed a total of 112 H75 Hawks to China, the 32 machines listed above represent the total given in the official "Aircraft Billing" book kept by the Curtiss-Wright Sales & Contract Division. However, these records show that William D. Pawley's Central Aircraft Manufacturing Corporation, operating in China at the time, was billed by C-W $557,540.00 for "one set of tools and materials for fixed-gear H75-M Hawks;" and Asian aircraft expert Richard Bueschel estimates this would have produced about 50 airplanes, giving China a total of 80-82 Hawk 75's, including General Chennault's H75-Q which had a P-36 retractable landing gear.

FINLAND

H75-A6		See Norway listing. Undetermined number of H75-A6's were captured by the Germans who sold eight to Finland

FRANCE

H75-A1	100 delivered	beginning 12/38; s/n (C-W) 12799 through 12897
H75-A2	100 delivered	beginning 5/39; s/n (C-W) 12932 through 13031
H75-A3	135 delivered	beginning 2/40 s/n (C-W) 13671 through 13805. Only a portion reached

| | | French forces before France fell; see text. |
| H75-A4 | 284 delivered | during 1940; s/n (C-W) 13806 and 13808 through 14090. Only six reached France; portion of this order to Great Britain, see below. |

GERMANY

| H75-A6 | | Germans seized an unknown number of the Hawk 75-A6's previously delivered to Norway when Germany occupied Norway 4/9/40; sold eight of these craft to Finland. |

GREAT BRITAIN

| Mohawk III | | See French order for H75-A3's. Britain obtained something less than 70 of these and about 50 were given RAF serials beginning with AR630. Twenty others carried RAF serials BK569 through BK588. |
| Mohawk IV | | See French order for H75-A4's. This French order was originally for 395 units, 174 of which had been built when France fell. Six reached France and 23 were diverted to Martinique. British accepted remaining 145, plus 110 additional for a total of 255. RAF retained 166 in Britain and sent 89 to India and South Africa. RAF serials were: BD918 through BD979 (62); BJ434 through BJ453 (20); BJ531 through BJ550 (20); BJ574 through BJ588 (15); BK876 through BK879 (4); BL220 through BL223 (4); BS730 through BS742 (13); BS784 through BS798 (15); BT470 through BT472 (3); LA157 through LA161 (5), plus five machines in the AR680 or AR690 serial range. |

INDIA

| H75-A5 | 5 delivered | beginning 8/42; serials unknown. Built by Pawley's Hindustan Aircraft, Ltd in Mysore, formerly Central Aircraft Manufacturing Corp in China. |

IRAN (PERSIA)

| H75-A9 | 10 delivered | beginning 3/41; s/n (C-W) 15252 through 15261. Captured in crates by the British who in turn sent them to India. |

NETHERLANDS EAST INDIES

| H75-A7 | 20 delivered | beginning 5/40; s/n (C-W) 14424 through 14443 |

NORWAY

| H75-A6 | 24 delivered | beginning 2/40; s/n (C-W) 13643 through 13654 and 13659 through 13670. |

| H75-A8 | 6 delivered | 2/41 to Norwegians in Canada. Serials unknown. Originally a 36-plane order but German occupation of Norway prevented delivery. Remaining 30 taken by USAAF (previously counted) as P-36G's. |

PERU

| P-36G | | See USAAF P-36G listing. Twenty-eight of these machines delivered to Peru in 1943 under Lend-Lease provisions. |

THAILAND (SIAM)

| H75-N | 12 delivered | 11 and 12/38; s/n (C-W) 12756 through 12767. |

Note: A 1946 company public relations publication, "C-W Airplane Model Designations," gives a total of 25 Hawk 75-N's sold to Thailand; but only the above 12 are listed in C-W Aircraft Billing.

778 TOTAL EXPORT HAWK 75's AND MOHAWKS (Does not include estimated 50 additional craft assembled in China by CAMCO).

U.S. Army Air Forces P-40 Models

A total of 13,738 Hawks of the P-40 series was built. Of these, 11,995 were delivered with USAAF serial numbers, though great numbers of these went directly to America's WW-II allies under provisions of the Lend-Lease Act. Tomahawk and Kittyhawk deliveries are listed separately, 1,741 of which were shipped directly from C-W without USAAF serials. The P-40's sent to the Soviet Union, both before and after Lend-Lease, all bore USAAF serials and are included below.

XP-40	1 delivered	10/38; s/n 38-010
P-40	199 delivered	beginning 6/40; s/n 39-156 through 39-220; 39-222 through 39-289, and 40-292 through 40-357 (20 to Russia).
P-40G	1 delivered	10/40; s/n 39-221. An additional 44 P-40G's were created when H81-A2 wings were fitted to 44 of the original P-40's listed above.
P-40B	131 delivered	beginning 1/41; s/n 41-5205 through 41-5304, and 41-13297 through 41-13327
P-40C	193 delivered	beginning 3/41; s/n 41-13328 through 41-13520
P-40D	22 delivered	7/41; s/n 40-359, and 40-361 through 40-381
XP-46	1 delivered	9/41; s/n 40-3053
XP-46A	1 delivered	9/41; s/n 40-3054
P-40E	820 delivered	beginning 8/41; s/n 40-358; 40-382 through 40-681; 41-5305 through 41-5744, and 41-13521 through 41-13599
P-40E-1	1,500 delivered	beginning 12/41; s/n 41-24766 through 41-25195, and 41-35874 through 41-36953

XP-40F	1 delivered	6/41; s/n 40-360. First Merlin-powered Hawk (P-40D airframe).
P-40F	699 delivered	beginning 1/42; s/n 41-13600 through 41-13695, and 41-13697 through 41-14299. The P-40F and subsequent P-40's were called "Warhawks."
P-40F-5	123 delivered	8/42; s/n 41-14300 through 41-14422
P-40F-10	177 delivered	10 and 11/42; s/n 41-14423 through 41-14599
P-40F-15	200 delivered	12/42; s/n 41-19733 through 41-19932
P-40F-20	112 delivered	1/43; s/n 41-19933 through 41-20044
P-40K-1	600 delivered	beginning 5/42; s/n 42-45722 through 42-46321
P-40K-5	200 delivered	9/42; s/n 42-9730 through 42-9929
P-40K-10	335 delivered	10 and 11/42; s/n 42-9930 through 42-10264
P-40K-15	165 delivered	11/42; s/n 42-10265 through 42-10429
P-40L-1	50 delivered	1/43; s/n 42-10430 through 42-10479
P-40L-5	220 delivered	1 and 2/43; s/n 42-10480 through 42-10699
P-40L-10	148 delivered	2 and 3/43; s/n 42-10700 through 42-10847
P-40L-15	112 delivered	3 and 4/43; s/n 42-10848 through 42-10959
P-40L-20	170 delivered	4/43; s/n 42-10960 through 42-11129
P-40M-1	60 delivered	11/42; s/n 43-5403 through 43-5462
P-40M-5	260 delivered	11 and 12/42; s/n 43-5464 through 43-5722
P-40M-10	280 delivered	1 and 2/43; s/n 43-5723 through 43-6002
P-40N-1	400 delivered	3 and 4/43; s/n 42-104429 through 42-104828. Fastest Warhawk at 378 mph.

P-40N-5	1,100 delivered	beginning 5/43; s/n 42-104829 through 42-105928
P-40N-10	100 delivered	8/43; s/n 42-105929 through 42-106028
P-40N-15	377 delivered	9/43; s/n 42-106029 through 42-106405
P-40N-20	1,523 delivered	beginning 9/43; s/n 42-106406 through 42-106428, and 43-22752 through 43-24251
P-40N-25	499 delivered	1 and 2/44; s/n 43-24252 through 43-24570, and 43-24572 through 43-24751
P-40N-30	500 delivered	beginning 4/44; s/n 44-7001 through 44-7500
P-40N-35	500 delivered	beginning 7/44; s/n 44-7501 through 44-8000
P-40N-40	216 delivered	beginning 10/44; s/n 44-47749 through 44-47964. This order for 1,000 units, but last 784 cancelled.
XP-40Q	1 delivered	6/44; s/n 43-24571
XP-40Q-1, -2 & -3		Conversions; P-40K-1 s/n 42-45722, and two P-40K-10's s/n 42-9987 and 42-10219.
P-40R-1 & P-40R-2		About 300 P-40F's and P-40L's in service were re-fitted with Allison engines due to Merlin parts shortage. P-40F's so modified were re-designated P-40R-1's; P-40L's receiving Allisons became P-40R-2's.

11,995 TOTAL P-40 MODELS DELIVERED TO USAAF

2 XP-46 and XP-46A DELIVERED TO USAAF

Note: USAAF Technical Order 01-1-81, dated 11/18/43, and revised 12/24/43, reclassified a number of early combat aircraft to "Restricted" status, meaning that these planes were "no longer considered entirely suitable to perform their primary combat missions, and will have their standard model symbols prefixed by the letter 'R'." Hawks listed were: RP-40, RP-40A, RP-40B, RP-40C, RP-40D and RP-40G.

Export Hawk 81 Models and Tomahawks

CHINA (AMERICAN VOLUNTEER GROUP)

H81-A2   100 delivered   beginning 5/41; s/n (C-W) random from 15337 to 15972 inclusive.

GREAT BRITAIN

Tomahawk Mk I, MK 1A & MK 1B (H81-A1)   142 delivered   beginning 9/40; s/n (RAF) BK852 and BK853; AH741 through AH880; Direct purchase; not Lend-Lease.

Tomahawk Mk II & Mk IIA (H81-A2)   110 delivered   10/30/40 through 11/27/40; s/n (RAF) AH881 through AH990. Not Lend-Lease.

Tomahawk MK IIB (H81-A2 & A3)   829 delivered   beginning 11/40; s/n (RAF) AH991 through AH999; AK100 through AK570; AM370 through AM519 (less 100 numbers reserved for planes, listed above, diverted to the AVG), and AN218 through AN517.

RUSSIA

P-40
Tomahawk MK II
Tomahawk MK IIB   The Soviets received 21 P-40's from the USAAF, random s/n 39-182 through 39-338, 7 and 10/40. Also 21 Tomahawk MK II from RAF and 49 Tomahawk IIB's from RAF.

1,081 TOTAL BRITISH EMPIRE TOMAHAWKS

100 TOTAL CHINESE (AVG) TOMAHAWKS

Export Model 87 Kittyhawks

GREAT BRITAIN

Kittyhawk MK I (H87-A2)   560 delivered   beginning 8/41; s/n (RAF) AK571 through AK999, and AL100 through AL230. Apparently Lend-Lease, but not delivered via USAAF and never given USAAF serials. L-L began 3/41.

Kittyhawk MK IA (H87-A3 & A4) (P-40E & E-1)	1,500 via L-L beginning 9/41; s/n (RAF) ET100 through ET999, and EV100 through EV699. These machines previously counted in USAAF listing.
Kittyhawk MK II (H87-B3) (P-40F & P-40L)	230 via L-L beginning 7/42; s/n (RAF) FL219 through FL488. These machines previously counted in USAAF listing.
Kittyhawk MK III (P-40M-5 &m-10) (P-40K)	364 via L-L beginning 11/42; s/n (RAF) FR210 through FR361; FR385 through FR392; FR412 through FR521, and FR779 through FR872. These craft previously counted in USAAF listing.
Kittyhawk MK IV (P-40N-1 through P-40N-35) (H87-V & H87-W)	458 via L-L beginning 3/43; s/n (RAF) FR884 and FR885; FT849 through FT 954 (FT898 through FT904 lost at sea), and FX498 through FX847. These craft previously counted in USAAF serial list).

560 TOTAL BRITISH KITTYHAWKS FROM CURTISS

(2,552) TOTAL BRITISH KITTYHAWKS, LEND-LEASE
(counted in previous USAAF totals)

USAAF & RAF P-40's and Kittyhawks Lend-Lease or transferred

AUSTRALIA	943	
BRAZIL	89	**Note:** These craft all originally bore
CANADA	360*	USAAF or RAF serials. *Estimate
NEW ZEALAND	293	based upon number of squadrons
FRANCE	61	known to have operated Kittyhawks.
SOUTH AFRICA	160*	
RUSSIA	2,091	

TOTAL HAWKS BUILT

U.S. Army biplanes, P-1 through XP/YP-23	247
Civilian biplanes (Gulfhawk & Essohawk)	2
U.S. Navy & Marine biplanes, F6C-1 through BF2C-1	157
Export biplanes, P-1 through Hawk IV	299
U.S. Army Air Corps P-36 series	241
U.S. Army Air Corps XP-42	1
Model 75 in civil license (demonstrators)	2
Export Model 75 and Mohawks	778
U.S. Army Air Corps XP/YP-37	14
USAAF P-40 series (includes Lend-Lease exports)	11,995
USAAF XP-46 and XP-46A	2
RAF Tomahawks (not Lend-Lease)	1,081
H81-A2 to China (American Volunteer Group)	100
Kittyhawks to Britain not given USAAF serials	560
TOTAL	**15,479**